The Scorcerer by Gilbert & Sullivan

Libretto by William S. Gilbert
Music by Arthur Sullivan

The partnership between William Schwenck Gilbert and Arthur Seymour Sullivan and their canon of Savoy Operas is rightly lauded by all lovers of comic opera the world over.

Gilbert's sharp, funny words and Sullivan's deliciously lively and hummable tunes create a world that is distinctly British in view but has the world as its audience.

Both men were exceptionally talented and gifted in their own right and wrote much, often with other partners, that still stands the test of time. However, together as a team they created Light or Comic Operas of a standard that have had no rivals equal to their standard, before or since. That's quite an achievement.

To be recognised by the critics is one thing but their commercial success was incredible. The profits were astronomical, allowing for the building of their own purpose built theatre – The Savoy Theatre.

Beginning with the first of their fourteen collaborations, Thespis in 1871 and travelling through many classics including The Sorcerer (1877), H.M.S. Pinafore (1878), The Pirates of Penzance (1879), The Mikado (1885), The Gondoliers (1889) to their finale in 1896 with The Grand Duke, Gilbert & Sullivan created a legacy that is constantly revived and admired in theatres and other media to this very day.

Index of Contents

The Sorcerer first appeared at the Opéra Comique, a little theatre on the Strand, on November 17, 1877. The original run was a 175 performances. It was enough to Gilbert & Sullivan to continue to collaborate,

DRAMATIS PERSONAE

Sir Marmaduke Pointdextre, an Elderly Baronet
Alexis, of the Grenadier Guards—His Son
Dr. Daly, Vicar of Ploverleigh
John Wellington Wells, of J. W. Wells & Co., Family Sorcerers
Lady Sangazure, a Lady of Ancient Lineage
Aline, Her Daughter—betrothed to Alexis

Mrs. Partlet, a Pew-Opener
Constance, her Daughter
Chorus of Villagers

ACT I.

SCENE—Exterior of Sir Marmaduke's Elizabethan Mansion, mid-day.

CHORUS OF VILLAGERS
Ring forth, ye bells,
With clarion sound—
Forget your knells,
For joys abound.
Forget your notes
Of mournful lay,
And from your throats
Pour joy to-day.

For to-day young Alexis—young Alexis Pointdextre
Is betrothed to Aline—to Aline Sangazure,
And that pride of his sex is—of his sex is to be next her
At the feast on the green—on the green, oh, be sure!

Ring forth, ye bells etc.

(Exeunt the MEN into house.)

(Enter MRS PARTLET with CONSTANCE, her daughter)

RECITATIVE

MRS PARTLET
Constance, my daughter, why this strange depression?
The village rings with seasonable joy,
Because the young and amiable Alexis,
Heir to the great Sir Marmaduke Pointdextre,
Is plighted to Aline, the only daughter
Of Annabella, Lady Sangazure.
You, you alone are sad and out of spirits;
What is the reason? Speak, my daughter, speak!

CONSTANCE

Oh, mother, do not ask! If my complexion
From red to white should change in quick succession,
And then from white to red, oh, take no notice!
If my poor limbs should tremble with emotion,
Pay no attention, mother—it is nothing!
If long and deep-drawn sighs I chance to utter,
Oh, heed them not, their cause must ne'er be known!

MRS PARTLET motions to CHORUS to leave her with CONSTANCE.

Exeunt LADIES OF CHORUS

ARIA—**CONSTANCE**

When he is here,
I sigh with pleasure—
When he is gone,
I sigh with grief.
My hopeless fear
No soul can measure—
His love alone
Can give my aching heart relief!

When he is cold,
I weep for sorrow—
When he is kind,
I weep for joy.
My grief untold
Knows no to-morrow—
My woe can find
No hope, no solace, no alloy!

MRS PARTLET

Come, tell me all about it! Do not fear—
I, too, have loved; but that was long ago!
Who is the object of your young affections?

CONSTANCE

Hush, mother! He is here! (Looking off)

Enter DR DALY. He is pensive and does not see them

MRS PARTLET (amazed)

Our reverend vicar!

CONSTANCE

Oh, pity me, my heart is almost broken!

MRS PARTLET
My child, be comforted. To such an union
I shall not offer any opposition.
Take him—he's yours! May you and he be happy!

CONSTANCE
But, mother dear, he is not yours to give!

MRS PARTLET
That's true, indeed!

CONSTANCE
He might object!

MRS PARTLET
He might.
But come—take heart—I'll probe him on the subject.
Be comforted—leave this affair to me.

(They withdraw.)

RECITATIVE—**DR. DALY**
The air is charged with amatory numbers—
Soft madrigals, and dreamy lovers' lays.
Peace, peace, old heart! Why waken from its slumbers
The aching memory of the old, old days?

BALLAD

Time was when Love and I were well acquainted.
Time was when we walked ever hand in hand.
A saintly youth, with worldly thought untainted,
None better-loved than I in all the land!
Time was, when maidens of the noblest station,
Forsaking even military men,
Would gaze upon me, rapt in adoration—
Ah me, I was a fair young curate then!

Had I a headache? sighed the maids assembled;
Had I a cold? welled forth the silent tear;
Did I look pale? then half a parish trembled;
And when I coughed all thought the end was near!
I had no care—no jealous doubts hung o'er me—
For I was loved beyond all other men.
Fled gilded dukes and belted earls before me—
Ah me, I was a pale young curate them!

(At the conclusion of the ballad, MRS PARTLET comes forward with CONSTANCE)

MRS PARTLET

Good day, reverend sir.

DR DALY

Ah, good Mrs. Partlet, I am glad to see you. And your little daughter, Constance! Why, she is quite a little woman, I declare!

CONSTANCE (aside)

Oh, mother, I cannot speak to him!

MRS PARTLET

Yes, reverend sir, she is nearly eighteen, and as good a girl as ever stepped. (Aside to Dr. Daly) Ah, sir, I'm afraid I shall soon lose her!

DR DALY (aside to Mrs. Partlet)

Dear me, you pain me very
much. Is she delicate?

MRS PARTLET

Oh no, sir—I don't mean that—but young girls look to get married.

DR DALY

Oh, I take you. To be sure. But there's plenty of time for that. Four or five years hence, Mrs. Partlet, four or five years hence. But when the time does come, I shall have much pleasure in marrying her myself—

CONSTANCE (aside)

Oh, mother!

DR DALY

To some strapping young fellow in her own rank of life.

CONSTANCE (in tears)

He does not love me!

MRS PARTLET

I have often wondered, reverend sir (if you'll excuse the liberty), that you have never married.

DR DALY (aside)

Be still, my fluttering heart!

MRS PARTLET

A clergyman's wife does so much good in a village. Besides that, you are not as young as you were, and before very long you will want somebody to nurse you, and look after your little comforts.

DR DALY

Mrs. Partlet, there is much truth in what you say. I am indeed getting on in years, and a helpmate would cheer my declining days. Time was when it might have been; but I have left it too long—I am an old fogy, now, am I not, my dear? (to CONSTANCE)—a very old fogy, indeed. Ha! ha! No, Mrs. Partlet, my mind is quite made up. I shall live and die a solitary old bachelor.

CONSTANCE
Oh, mother, mother!

(Sobs on Mrs. PARTLET'S bosom)

MRS PARTLET
Come, come, dear one, don't fret. At a more fitting time we will try again—we will try again.

(Exeunt Mrs. Partlet and Constance.)

DR DALY (looking after them)
Poor little girl! I'm afraid she has something on her mind. She is rather comely. Time was when this old heart would have throbbed in double-time at the sight of such a fairy form! But tush! I am puling! Here comes the young Alexis with his proud and happy father. Let me dry this tell-tale tear!

Enter SIR MARMADUKE and ALEXIS

RECITATIVE

DR DALY
Sir Marmaduke—my dear young friend, Alexis—
On this most happy, most auspicious plighting—
Permit me as a true old friend to tender
My best, my very best congratulations!

SIR MARMADUKE
Sir, you are most obleeging!

ALEX.
Dr. Daly
My dear old tutor, and my valued pastor,
I thank you from the bottom of my heart!

(Spoken through music)

DR DALY
May fortune bless you! may the middle distance
Of your young life be pleasant as the foreground—
The joyous foreground! and, when you have reached it,
May that which now is the far-off horizon
(But which will then become the middle distance),
In fruitful promise be exceeded only
By that which will have opened, in the meantime,

Into a new and glorious horizon!

SIR MARMADUKE
Dear Sir, that is an excellent example
Of an old school of stately compliment
To which I have, through life, been much addicted.
Will you obleege me with a copy of it,
In clerkly manuscript, that I myself
May use it on appropriate occasions?

DR DALY
Sir, you shall have a fairly-written copy
Ere Sol has sunk into his western slumbers!

(Exit DR DALY)

SIR MARMADUKE (to ALEXIS, who is in a reverie)
Come, come, my son—your fiancee will be here in five minutes. Rouse yourself to receive her.

ALEXIS
Oh rapture!

SIR MARMADUKE
Yes, you are a fortunate young fellow, and I will not disguise from you that this union with the House of Sangazure realizes my fondest wishes. Aline is rich, and she comes of a sufficiently old family, for she is the seven thousand and thirty-seventh in direct descent from Helen of Troy. True, there was a blot on the escutcheon of that lady—that affair with Paris—but where is the family, other than my own, in which there is no flaw? You are a lucky fellow, sir—a very lucky fellow!

ALEXIS
Father, I am welling over with limpid joy! No sicklying taint of sorrow overlies the lucid lake of liquid love, upon which, hand in hand, Aline and I are to float into eternity!

SIR MARMADUKE
Alexis, I desire that of your love for this young lady you do not speak so openly. You are always singing ballads in praise of her beauty, and you expect the very menials who wait behind your chair to chorus your ecstasies. It is not delicate.

ALEXIS
Father, a man who loves as I love—

SIR MARMADUKE
Pooh pooh, sir! fifty years ago I madly loved your future mother-in-law, the Lady Sangazure, and I have reason to believe that she returned my love. But were we guilty of the indelicacy of publicly rushing into each other's arms, exclaiming—

"Oh, my adored one!" "Beloved boy!"
"Ecstatic rapture!" "Unmingled joy!"

which seems to be the modern fashion of love-making? No! it was "Madam, I trust you are in the enjoyment of good health"—"Sir, you are vastly polite, I protest I am mighty well"—and so forth. Much more delicate—much more respectful. But see—Aline approaches—let us retire, that she may compose herself for the interesting ceremony in which she is to play so important a part.

(Exeunt SIR MARMADUKE and ALEXIS)

(Enter ALINE on terrace, preceded by CHORUS OF GIRLS)

CHORUS OF GIRLS
With heart and with voice
Let us welcome this mating:
To the youth of her choice,
With a heart palpitating,
Comes the lovely Aline!

May their love never cloy!
May their bliss me unbounded!
With a halo of joy
May their lives be surrounded!
Heaven bless our Aline!

RECITATIVE—**ALINE**.
My kindly friends, I thank you for this greeting
And as you wish me every earthly joy,
I trust your wishes may have quick fulfillment!

ARIA—**ALINE**.
Oh, happy young heart!
Comes thy young lord a-wooing
With joy in his eyes,
And pride in his breast—
Make much of thy prize,
For he is the best
That ever came a-suing.
Yet—yet we must part,
Young heart!
Yet—yet we must part!

Oh, merry young heart,
Bright are the days of thy wooing!
But happier far
The days untried—
No sorrow can mar,
When love has tied
The knot there's no undoing.
Then, never to part,

Young heart!
Then, never to part!

Enter LADY SANGAZURE

RECITATIVE—**LADY SANGAZURE**
My child, I join in these congratulations:
Heed not the tear that dims this aged eye!
Old memories crowd upon me. Though I sorrow,
'Tis for myself, Aline, and not for thee!

Enter ALEXIS, preceded by CHORUS OF MEN

CHORUS OF MEN AND WOMEN
With heart and with voice
Let us welcome this mating;
To the maid of his choice,
With a heart palpitating,
Comes Alexis, the brave!.

(SIR MARMADUKE enters. LADY SANGAZURE and he exhibit signs of strong emotion at the sight of each
other which they endeavor to repress. ALEXIS and ALINE rush into each other's arms.)

RECITATIVE

ALEXIS
Oh, my adored one!

ALINE
Beloved boy!

ALEXIS
Ecstatic rapture!

ALINE
Unmingled joy!

(They retire up.)

DUET—**SIR MARMADUKE and LADY SANGAZURE**

SIR MARMADUKE (with stately courtesy)
Welcome joy, adieu to sadness!
As Aurora gilds the day,
So those eyes, twin orbs of gladness,
Chase the clouds of care away.
Irresistible incentive
Bids me humbly kiss your hand;

I'm your service most attentive—
Most attentive to command!

(Aside with frantic vehemence)
Wild with adoration!
Mad with fascination!
To indulge my lamentation
No occasion do I miss!
Goaded to distraction
By maddening inaction,
I find some satisfaction
In apostophe like this:
"Sangazure immortal,
"Sangazure divine,
"Welcome to my portal,
"Angel, oh be mine!"

(Aloud with much ceremony)

Irresistible incentive
Bids me humbly kiss your hand;
I'm your servant most attentive—
Most attentive to command!

LADY SANGAZURE
Sir, I thank you most politely
For your grateful courtesee;
Compliment more true and knightly
Never yet was paid to me!
Chivalry is an ingredient
Sadly lacking in our land—
Sir, I am your most obedient,
Most obedient to command!

(Aside and with great vehemence)
Wild with adoration!
Mad with fascination!
To indulge my lamentation
No occasion do I miss!
Goaded to distraction
By maddening inaction,
I find some satisfaction
In apostophe like this:
"Marmaduke immortal,
"Marmaduke divine,
"Take me to thy portal,
"Loved one, oh be mine!"

(Aloud with much ceremony)
Chivalry is an ingredient
Sadly lacking in our land;
Sir, I am your most obedient,
Most obedient to command!

(During this the NOTARY has entered, with marriage contract.)

RECITATIVE—**NOTARY**
All is prepared for sealing and for signing,
The contract has been drafted as agreed;
Approach the table, oh, ye lovers pining,
With hand and seal come execute the deed!

(ALEXIS and ALINE advance and sign, ALEXIS supported by SIR MARMADUKE, ALINE by her MOTHER)

CHORUS
See they sign, without a quiver, it—
Then to seal proceed.
They deliver it—they deliver it
As their Act and Deed!

ALEXIS
I deliver it—I deliver it
As my Act and Deed!.

ALINE.
I deliver it—I deliver it.
As my Act and Deed!

CHORUS
With heart and with voice
Let us welcome this mating;
Leave them here to rejoice,
With true love palpitating,
Alexis the brave,
And the lovely Aline!

(Exeunt all but ALEXIS and ALINE)

ALEXIS
At last we are alone! My darling, you are now irrevocably betrothed to me. Are you not very, very happy?

ALINE
Oh, Alexis, can you doubt it? Do I not love you beyond all on earth, and am I not beloved in return? Is not true love, faithfully given and faithfully returned, the source of every earthly joy?

ALEXIS

Of that there can be no doubt. Oh, that the world could be persuaded of the truth of that maxim! Oh, that the world would break down the artificial barriers of rank, wealth, education, age, beauty, habits, taste, and temper, and recognize the glorious principle, that in marriage alone is to be found the panacea for every ill!

ALINE

Continue to preach that sweet doctrine, and you will succeed, oh, evangel of true happiness!

ALEXIS

I hope so, but as yet the cause progresses but slowly. Still I have made some converts to the principle, that men and women should be coupled in matrimony without distinction of rank. I have lectured on the subject at Mechanics' Institutes, and the mechanics were unanimous in favour of my views. I have preached in workhouses, beershops, and Lunatic Asylums, and I have been received with enthusiasm. I have addressed navvies on the advantages that would accrue to them if they married wealthy ladies of rank, and not a navvy dissented!

ALINE

Noble fellows! And yet there are those who hold that the uneducated classes are not open to argument! And what do the countesses say?

ALEXIS

Why, at present, it can't be denied, the aristocracy hold aloof.

ALINE

Ah, the working man is the true Intelligence after all!

ALEXIS

He is a noble creature when he is quite sober. Yes, Aline, true happiness comes of true love, and true love should be independent of external influences. It should live upon itself and by itself—in itself love should live for love alone!

BALLAD—**ALEXIS**
Love feeds on many kinds of food, I know,
Some love for rank, some for duty:
Some give their hearts away for empty show,
And others for youth and beauty.
To love for money all the world is prone:
Some love themselves, and live all lonely:
Give me the love that loves for love alone—
I love that love—I love it only!

What man for any other joy can thirst,
Whose loving wife adores him duly?
Want, misery, and care may do their worst,
If loving woman loves you truly.
A lover's thoughts are ever with his own—
None truly loved is ever lonely:

Give me the love that loves for love alone—
I love that love—I love it only!

ALINE
Oh, Alexis, those are noble principles!

ALEXIS
Yes, Aline, and I am going to take a desperate step in support of them. Have you ever heard of the firm of J. W. Wells & Co., the old-established Family Sorcerers in St. Mary Axe?

ALINE
I have seen their advertisement.

ALEXIS
They have invented a philtre, which, if report may be believed, is simply infallible. I intend to distribute it through the village, and within half an hour of my doing so there will not be an adult in the place who will not have learnt the secret of pure and lasting happiness. What do you say to that?

ALINE
Well, dear, of course a filter is a very useful thing in a house; but still I don't quite see that it is the sort of thing that places its possessor on the very pinnacle of earthly joy.

ALEXIS
Aline, you misunderstand me. I didn't say a filter—I said a philtre.

ALINE (alarmed)
You don't mean a love-potion?

ALEXIS
On the contrary—I do mean a love potion.

ALINE
Oh, Alexis! I don't think it would be right. I don't indeed. And then—a real magician! Oh, it would be downright wicked.

ALEXIS
Aline, is it, or is it not, a laudable object to steep the whole village up to its lips in love, and to couple them in matrimony without distinction of age, rank, or fortune?

ALINE
Unquestionably, but—

ALEXIS
Then unpleasant as it must be to have recourse to supernatural aid, I must nevertheless pocket my aversion, in deference to the great and good end I have in view. (Calling) Hercules.

(Enter a PAGE from tent)

PAGE
Yes, sir.

ALEXIS
Is Mr. Wells there?

PAGE
He's in the tent, sir—refreshing.

ALEXIS
Ask him to be so good as to step this way.

PAGE
Yes, sir.

(Exit PAGE)

ALINE
Oh, but, Alexis! A real Sorcerer! Oh, I shall be frightened to death!

ALEXIS
I trust my Aline will not yield to fear while the strong right arm of her Alexis is here to protect her.

ALINE
It's nonsense, dear, to talk of your protecting me with your strong right arm, in face of the fact that this Family Sorcerer could change me into a guinea-pig before you could turn round.

ALEXIS
He could change you into a guinea-pig, no doubt, but it is most unlikely that he would take such a liberty. It's a most respectable firm, and I am sure he would never be guilty of so untradesmanlike an act.

(Enter MR WELLS from tent)

MR WELLS
Good day, sir. (ALINE much terrified.)

ALEXIS
Good day—I believe you are a Sorcerer.

MR WELLS
Yes, sir, we practice Necromancy in all its branches. We've a choice assortment of wishing-caps, divining-rods, amulets, charms, and counter-charms. We can cast you a nativity at a low figure, and we have a horoscope at three-and-six that we can guarantee. Our Abudah chests, each containing a patent Hag who comes out and prophesies disasters, with spring complete, are strongly recommended. Our Aladdin lamps are very chaste, and our Prophetic Tablets, foretelling everything—from a change of Ministry down to a rise in Unified—are much enquired for. Our penny Curse—one of the cheapest

things in the trade—is considered infallible. We have some very superior Blessings, too, but they're very little asked for. We've only sold one since Christmas—to a gentleman who bought it to send to his mother-in-law—but it turned out that he was afflicted in the head, and it's been returned on our hands. But our sale of penny Curses, especially on Saturday nights, is tremendous. We can't turn 'em out fast enough.

SONG—**MR. WELLS**
Oh! my name is John Wellington Wells,
I'm a dealer in magic and spells,
In blessings and curses
And ever-filled purses,
In prophecies, witches, and knells.
If you want a proud foe to "make tracks"—
If you'd melt a rich uncle in wax—
You've but to look in
On the resident Djinn,
Number seventy, Simmery Axe!

We've a first-class assortment of magic;
And for raising a posthumous shade
With effects that are comic or tragic,
There's no cheaper house in the trade.
Love-philtre—we've quantities of it;
And for knowledge if any one burns,
We keep an extremely small prophet, a prophet
Who brings us unbounded returns:

For he can prophesy
With a wink of his eye,
Peep with security
Into futurity,
Sum up your history,
Clear up a mystery,
Humour proclivity
For a nativity—for a nativity;
With mirrors so magical,
Tetrapods tragical,
Bogies spectacular,
Answers oracular,
Facts astronomical,
Solemn or comical,
And, if you want it, he
Makes a reduction on taking a quantity!
Oh!

If any one anything lacks,
He'll find it all ready in stacks,
If he'll only look in

On the resident Djinn,
Number seventy, Simmery Axe!

He can raise you hosts
Of ghosts,
And that without reflectors;
And creepy things
With wings,
And gaunt and grisly spectres.
He can fill you crowds
Of shrouds,
And horrify you vastly;
He can rack your brains
With chains,
And gibberings grim and ghastly.

And then, if you plan it, he
Changes organity,
With an urbanity,
Full of Satanity,
Vexes humanity
With an inanity
Fatal to vanity—
Driving your foes to the verge of insanity!

Barring tautology,
In demonology,
'Lectro-biology,
Mystic nosology,
Spirit philology,
High-class astrology,
Such is his knowledge, he
Isn't the man to require an apology!

Oh!
My name is John Wellington Wells,
I'm a dealer in magic and spells,
In blessings and curses
And ever-filled purses,
In prophecies, witches, and knells.

If any one anything lacks,
He'll find it all ready in stacks,
If he'll only look in
On the resident Djinn,
Number seventy, Simmery Axe!

ALEXIS

I have sent for you to consult you on a very important matter. I believe you advertise a Patent Oxy-Hydrogen Love-at-first-sight Philtre?

MR WELLS
Sir, it is our leading article. (Producing a phial.)

ALEXIS
Now I want to know if you can confidently guarantee it as possessing all the qualities you claim for it in your advertisement?

MR WELLS
Sir, we are not in the habit of puffing our goods. Ours is an old-established house with a large family connection, and every assurance held out in the advertisement is fully realized. (Hurt)

ALINE (aside)
Oh, Alexis, don't offend him! He'll change us into something dreadful—I know he will!

ALEXIS
I am anxious from purely philanthropical motives to distribute this philtre, secretly, among the inhabitants of this village. I shall of course require a quantity. How do you sell it?

MR WELLS
In buying a quantity, sir, we should strongly advise your taking it in the wood, and drawing it off as you happen to want it. We have it in four-and-a-half and nine gallon casks—also in pipes and hogsheads for laying down, and we deduct 10 per cent from prompt cash.

ALEXIS
I should mention that I am a Member of the Army and Navy Stores.

MR WELLS
In that case we deduct 25 percent.

ALEXIS
Aline, the villagers will assemble to carouse in a few minutes. Go and fetch the tea-pot.

ALINE
But, Alexis—

ALEXIS
My dear, you must obey me, if you please. Go and fetch the teapot.

ALINE (going)
I'm sure Dr. Daly would disapprove of it!

(Exit ALINE.)

ALEXIS
And how soon does it take effect?

MR WELLS
In twelve hours. Whoever drinks of it loses consciousness for that period, and on waking falls in love, as a matter of course, with the first lady he meets who has also tasted it, and his affection is at once returned. One trial will prove the fact.

Enter ALINE with large tea-pot

ALEXIS
Good: then, Mr. Wells, I shall feel obliged if you will at once pour as much philtre into this teapot as will suffice to affect the whole village.

ALINE
But bless me, Alexis, many of the villages are married people!

MR WELLS
Madam, this philtre is compounded on the strictest principles. On married people it has no effect whatever. But are you quite sure that you have nerve enough to carry you through the fearful ordeal?

ALEXIS
In the good cause I fear nothing.

MR WELLS
Very good, then, we will proceed at once to the Incantation.

The stage grows dark.

INCANTATION

MR WELLS
Sprites of earth and air—
Fiends of flame and fire—
Demon souls,
Come here in shoals,
This dreaded deed inspire!
Appear, appear, appear.

MALE VOICES
Good master, we are here!

MR WELLS
Noisome hags of night—
Imps of deadly shade—
Pallid ghosts,
Arise in hosts,
And lend me all your aid.
Appear, appear, appear!

FEMALE VOICES
Good master, we are here!

ALEXIS (aside)
Hark, they assemble,
These fiends of the night!

ALINE (aside)
Oh Alexis, I tremble,
Seek safety in flight!

ARIA — **ALINE**
Let us fly to a far-off land,
Where peace and plenty dwell—
Where the sigh of the silver strand
Is echoed in every shell
To the joy that land will give,
On the wings of Love we'll fly;
In innocence, there to live—
In innocence there to die!

CHORUS OF SPIRITS
Too late—too late
It may not be!
That happy fate
Is not for (me/thee)!

ALEXIS, ALINE, and MR WELLS
Too late—too late,
That may not be!
That happy fate,
Is not for thee!

MR WELLS
Now shrivelled hags, with poison bags,
Discharge your loathsome loads!
Spit flame and fire, unholy choir!
Belch forth your venom, toads!
Ye demons fell, with yelp and yell,
Shed curses far afield—
Ye fiends of night, your filthy blight
In noisome plenty yield!

MR WELLS (pouring phial into tea-pot—flash)
Number One!

CHORUS
It is done!

MR WELLS (same business)
Number Two!

(flash)

CHORUS
One too few!

MR WELLS
Number Three!

(flash)

CHORUS
Set us free!
Set us free-our work is done
Ha! ha! ha!
Set us free—our course is run!
Ha! ha! ha!

ALINE AND ALEXIS (aside)
Let us fly to a far-off land,
Where peace and plenty dwell—
Where the sigh of the silver strand
Is echoed in every shell.

CHORUS OF FIENDS.
Ha! ha! ha! ha! ha! ha! ha! ha! ha! ha!

(Stage grows light. MR WELLS beckons VILLAGERS. Enter VILLAGERS and all the dramatis personae, dancing joyously. MRS APRTLET and MR WELLS then distribute tea-cups.)

CHORUS
Now to the banquet we press;
Now for the eggs, the ham;
Now for the mustard and cress,
Now for the strawberry jam!

Now for the tea of our host,
Now for the rollicking bun,
Now for the muffin and toast,
Now for the gay Sally Lunn!

WOMEN
The eggs and the ham, and the strawberry jam!

MEN

The rollicking bun, and the gay Sally Lunn!
The rollicking, rollicking bun!

RECITATIVE—**SIR MARMADUKE**
Be happy all—the feast is spread before ye;
Fear nothing, but enjoy yourselves, I pray!
Eat, aye, and drink—be merry, I implore ye,
For once let thoughtless Folly rule the day.

TEA-CUP BRINDISI
Eat, drink, and be gay,
Banish all worry and sorrow,
Laugh gaily to-day,
Weep, if you're sorry, to-morrow!
Come, pass the cup around—
I will go bail for the liquor;
It's strong, I'll be bound,
For it was brewed by the vicar!

CHORUS
None so knowing as he
At brewing a jorum of tea,
Ha! ha!
A pretty stiff jorum of tea.

TRIO—**MR WELLS, ALINE, and ALEXIS** (aside)
See—see—they drink—
All thoughts unheeding,
The tea-cups clink,
They are exceeding!
Their hearts will melt
In half-an-hour—
Then will be felt
The potions power!

(During this verse CONSTANCE has brought a small tea-pot, kettle, caddy, and cosy to DR DALY. He makes tea scientifically.)

BRINDISI, 2nd Verse—DR. DALY (with the tea-pot)
Pain, trouble, and care,
Misery, heart-ache, and worry,
Quick, out of your lair!
Get you gone in a hurry!
Toil, sorrow, and plot,
Fly away quicker and quicker—
Three spoons in the pot—
That is the brew of your vicar!

CHORUS

None so cunning as he
At brewing a jorum of tea,
Ha! ha!
A pretty stiff jorum of tea!

ENSEMBLE—**ALEXIS and ALINE** (aside)

Oh love, true love—unworldly, abiding!
Source of all pleasure—true fountain of joy,—
Oh love, true love—divinely confiding,
Exquisite treasure that knows no alloy,—
Oh love, true love, rich harvest of gladness,
Peace-bearing tillage—great garner of bliss,—
Oh love, true love, look down on our sadness —
Dwell in this village—oh, hear us in this!

(It becomes evident by the strange conduct of the characters that the charm is working. All rub their eyes, and stagger about the stage as if under the influence of a narcotic.)

TUTTI (aside)	**ALEXIS, MR. WELLS and ALINE**
Oh, marvellous illusion!	A marvellous illusion!
Oh, terrible surprise!	A terrible surprise
What is this strange confusion	Excites a strange confusion
That veils my aching eyes?	Within their aching eyes—
I must regain my senses,	They must regain their senses,
Restoring Reason's law,	Restoring Reason's law,
Or fearful inferences	Or fearful inferences
Society will draw!	Society will draw!

(Those who have partaken of the philtre struggle in vain against its effects, and, at the end of the chorus, fall insensible on the stage.)

END OF ACT I

Scene—Exterior of SIR MARMADUKE'S mansion by moonlight.

All the PEASANTRY are discovered asleep on the ground, as at the end of Act I.

Enter MR WELLS, on tiptoe, followed by ALEXIS and ALINE. MR WELLS carries a dark lantern.

TRIO—**ALEXIS, ALINE, and MR WELLS**

'Tis twelve, I think,
And at this mystic hour

The magic drink
Should manifest its power.
Oh, slumbering forms,
How little ye have guessed
That fire that warms
Each apathetic breast!

ALEXIS
But stay, my father is not here!

ALINE
And pray where is my mother dear?

MR WELLS
I did not think it meet to see
A dame of lengthy pedigree,
A Baronet and K.C.B.
A Doctor of Divinity,
And that respectable Q.C.,
All fast asleep, al-fresco-ly,
And so I had them taken home
And put to bed respectably!
I trust my conduct meets your approbation.

ALEXIS
Sir, you have acted with discrimination,
And shown more delicate appreciation
Than we expect of persons of your station.

MR WELLS
But stay—they waken one by one —
The spell has worked—the deed is done!
I would suggest that we retire
While Love, the Housemaid, lights her kitchen fire!

(Exeunt MR WELLS, ALEXIS and ALINE, on tiptoe, as the villagers stretch their arms, yawn, rub their eyes, and sit up.)

MEN
Why, where be oi, and what be oi a doin',
A sleepin' out, just when the dews du rise?

GIRLS
Why, that's the very way your health to ruin,
And don't seem quite respectable likewise!

MEN (staring at girls)
Eh, that's you!

Only think o' that now!

GIRLS (coyly)
What may you be at, now?
Tell me, du!

MEN (admiringly)
Eh, what a nose,
And eh, what eyes, miss!
Lips like a rose,
And cheeks likewise, miss!

GIRLS (coyly)
Oi tell you true,
Which I've never done, sir,
Oi loike you
As I never loiked none, sir!

ALL
Eh, but oi du loike you!

MEN
If you'll marry me, I'll dig for you and rake for you!

GIRLS
If you'll marry be, I'll scrub for you and bake for you!

MEN
If you'll marry me, all others I'll forsake for you!

ALL
All this will I du, if you marry me!

GIRLS
If you'll marry me, I'll cook for you and brew for you!

MEN
If you'll marry me, I've guineas not a few for you!
GIRLS
If you'll marry me, I'll take you in and du for you!

ALL
All this will I du, if you'll marry me!
Eh, but I do loike you!

Country Dance

(At end of dance, enter CONSTANCE in tears, leading NOTARY, who carries an ear-trumpet)

Aria—**CONSTANCE**

Dear friends, take pity on my lot,
My cup is not of nectar!
I long have loved—as who would not?—
Our kind and reverend rector.
Long years ago my love began
So sweetly—yet so sadly—
But when I saw this plain old man,
Away my old affection ran—
I found I loved him madly.
Oh!

(To NOTARY)
You very, very plain old man,
I love, I love you madly!

CHORUS

You very, very plain old man,
She loves, she loves you madly!

NOTARY

I am a very deaf old man,
And hear you very badly!

CONSTANCE

I know not why I love him so;
It is enchantment, surely!
He's dry and snuffy, deaf and slow
Ill-tempered, weak and poorly!
He's ugly, and absurdly dressed,
And sixty-seven nearly,
He's everything that I detest,
But if the truth must be confessed,
I love him very dearly!
Oh!

(To NOTARY)
You're everything that I detest,
But still I love you dearly!

CHORUS

You've everything that girls detest,
But still she loves you dearly!

NOTARY

I caught that line, but for the rest,
I did not hear it clearly!

(During this verse ALINE and ALEXIS have entered at back unobserved.)

ALINE AND ALEXIS

ALEX
Oh joy! oh joy!
The charm works well,
And all are now united.

ALINE.
The blind young boy
Obeys the spell,
And troth they all have plighted!

ENSEMBLE

Aline & Alexis	Constance	Notary
Oh joy! oh joy!	Oh, bitter joy!	Oh joy! Oh joy!
The charm works well,	No words can tell	No words can tell
And all are now united!	How my poor heart	My state of mind
The blind young boy	is blighted!	delighted.
Obeys the spell,	They'll soon employ	They'll soon employ
A marriage bell,	A marriage bell,	
Their troth they all	To say that we're	To say that we're
have plighted.	united.	united.
True happiness	I do confess	True happiness
Reigns everywhere,	A sorrow rare	Reigns everywhere
And dwells with both	My humbled spirit	And dwells with both
the sexes.	vexes.	The sexes,
And all will bless	And none will bless	And all will bless
The thoughtful care	Example rare	Example rare
Of their beloved	Of their beloved	Of their beloved
Alexis!	Alexis!	Alexis!

(All, except ALEXIS and ALINE, exeunt lovingly.)

ALINE
How joyful they all seem in their new-found happiness! The whole village has paired off in the happiest manner. And yet not a match has been made that the hollow world would not consider ill-advised!

ALEXIS
But we are wiser—far wiser—than the world. Observe the good that will become of these ill-assorted unions. The miserly wife will check the reckless expenditure of her too frivolous consort, the wealthy husband will shower innumerable bonnets on his penniless bride, and the young and lively spouse will cheer the declining days of her aged partner with comic songs unceasing!

ALINE

What a delightful prospect for him!

ALEXIS

But one thing remains to be done, that my happiness may be complete. We must drink the philtre ourselves, that I may be assured of your love for ever and ever.

ALINE

Oh, Alexis, do you doubt me? Is it necessary that such love as ours should be secured by artificial means? Oh, no, no, no!

ALEXIS

My dear Aline, time works terrible changes, and I want to place our love beyond the chance of change.

ALINE

Alexis, it is already far beyond that chance. Have faith in me, for my love can never, never change!

ALEXIS

Then you absolutely refuse?

ALINE

I do. If you cannot trust me, you have no right to love me—no right to be loved by me.

ALEXIS

Enough, Aline, I shall know how to interpret this refusal.

BALLAD—**ALEXIS**
Thou hast the power thy vaunted love
To sanctify, all doubt above,
Despite the gathering shade:
To make that love of thine so sure
That, come what may, it must endure
Till time itself shall fade.
They love is but a flower
That fades within the hour!
If such thy love, oh, shame!
Call it by other name—
It is not love!

Thine is the power and thine alone,
To place me on so proud a throne
That kings might envy me!
A priceless throne of love untold,
More rare than orient pearl and gold.
But no! Thou wouldst be free!
Such love is like the ray
That dies within the day:
If such thy love, oh, shame!
Call it by other name—

It is not love!

Enter DR DALY

DR DALY (musing)
It is singular—it is very singular. It has overthrown all my calculations. It is distinctly opposed to the doctrine of averages. I cannot understand it.

ALINE
Dear Dr. Daly, what has puzzled you?

DR DALY
My dear, this village has not hitherto been addicted to marrying and giving in marriage. Hitherto the youths of this village have not been enterprising, and the maidens have been distinctly coy. Judge then of my surprise when I tell you that the whole village came to me in a body just now, and implored me to join them in matrimony with as little delay as possible. Even your excellent father has hinted to me that before very long it is not unlikely that he may also change his condition.

ALINE
Oh, Alexis—do you hear that? Are you not delighted?

ALEXIS
Yes, I confess that a union between your mother and my father would be a happy circumstance indeed. (Crossing to DR DALY) My dear sir—the news that you bring us is very gratifying.

DR DALY
Yes—still, in my eyes, it has its melancholy side.

This universal marrying recalls the happy days—now, alas, gone forever—when I myself might have—but tush! I am puling. I am too old to marry—and yet, within the last half-hour, I have greatly yearned for companionship. I never remarked it before, but the young maidens of this village are very comely. So likewise are the middle-aged. Also the elderly. All are comely—and (with a deep sigh) all are engaged!

ALINE
Here comes your father.

Enter SIR MARMADUKE with MRS PARTLET, arm-in-arm

ALINE and ALEXIS (aside).
Mrs. Partlet!

SIR MARMADUKE
Dr. Daly, give me joy. Alexis, my dear boy, you will, I am sure, be pleased to hear that my declining days are not unlikely to be solaced by the companionship of this good, virtuous, and amiable woman.

ALEXIS (rather taken aback)

My dear father, this is not altogether what I expected. I am certainly taken somewhat by surprise. Still it can hardly be necessary to assure you that any wife of yours is a mother of mine. (Aside to Aline.) It is not quite what I could have wished.

MRS PARTLET (crossing to Alexis)
Oh, sir, I entreat your forgiveness. I am aware that socially I am not everything that could be desired, nor am I blessed with an abundance of worldly goods, but I can at least confer on your estimable father the great and priceless dowry of a true, tender, and lovin' 'art!

ALEXIS (coldly)
I do not question it. After all, a faithful love is the true source of every earthly joy.

SIR MARMADUKE
I knew that my boy would not blame his poor father for acting on the impulse of a heart that has never yet misled him. Zorah is not perhaps what the world calls beautiful—

DR DALY
Still she is comely—distinctly comely. (Sighs)

ALINE
Zorah is very good, and very clean, and honest, and quite, quite sober in her habits: and that is worth far more than beauty, dear Sir Marmaduke.

DR DALY
Yes; beauty will fade and perish, but personal cleanliness is practically undying, for it can be renewed whenever it discovers symptoms of decay. My dear Sir Marmaduke, I heartily congratulate you. (Sighs)

QUINTETTE

ALEXIS, ALINE, SIR MARMADUKE, ZORAH, and DR. DALY

ALEXIS.
I rejoice that it's decided,
Happy now will be his life,
For my father is provided
With a true and tender wife.
She will tend him, nurse him, mend him,
Air his linen, dry his tears;
Bless the thoughtful fate that send him
Such a wife to soothe his years!

ALINE.
No young giddy thoughtless maiden,
Full of graces, airs, and jeers—
But a sober widow, laden
With the weight of fifty years!

SIR MARMADUKE

No high-born exacting beauty
Blazing like a jewelled sun—
But a wife who'll do her duty,
As that duty should be done!

MRS PARTLET
I'm no saucy minx and giddy—
Hussies such as them abound—
But a clean and tidy widdy
Well be-known for miles around!

DR DALY
All the village now have mated,
All are happy as can be—
I to live alone am fated:
No one's left to marry me!

ENSEMBLE
She will tend him etc.

(Exeunt SIR MARMADUKE, MRS PARTLET, and ALINE, with ALEXIS. DR DALY looks after them sentimentally, then exits with a sigh.)

Enter MR WELLS

RECITATIVE—**MR WELLS**
Oh, I have wrought much evil with my spells!
And ill I can't undo!
This is too bad of you, J. W. Wells—
What wrong have they done you?
And see—another love-lorn lady comes—
Alas, poor stricken dame!
A gentle pensiveness her life benumbs—
And mine, alone, the blame!

LADY SANGAZURE enters. She is very melancholy

LADY SANGAZURE
Alas, ah me! and well-a-day!
I sigh for love, and well I may,
For I am very old and grey.
But stay!

(Sees MR WELLS, and becomes fascinated by him.)

RECITATIVE

LADY SANGAZURE

What is this fairy form I see before me?

MR WELLS
Oh horrible!—She's going to adore me!
This last catastrophe is overpowering!

LADY SANGAZURE
Why do you glare at one with visage lowering?
For pity's sake recoil not thus from me!

MR WELLS
My lady leave me—this may never be!

DUET—**LADY SANGAZURE and MR WELLS**

MR WELLS
Hate me! I drop my H's—have through life!

LADY SANGAZURE
Love me! I'll drop them too!

MR WELLS
Hate me! I always eat peas with a knife!

LADY SANGAZURE
Love me! I'll eat like you!

MR WELLS
Hate me! I spend the day at Rosherville!

LADY SANGAZURE
Love me! that joy I'll share!

MR WELLS
Hate me! I often roll down One Tree Hill!

LADY SANGAZURE
Love me! I'll join you there!

LADY SANGAZURE
Love me! My prejudices I will drop!

MR WELLS
Hate me! that's not enough!

LADY SANGAZURE
Love me! I'll come and help you in the shop!

MR WELLS
Hate me! the life is rough!

LADY SANGAZURE
Love me! my grammar I will all forswear!

MR WELLS
Hate me! abjure my lot!

LADY SANGAZURE
Love me! I'll stick sunflowers in my hair!

MR WELLS
Hate me! they'll suit you not!

RECITATIVE—**MR. WELLS**
At what I am going to say be not enraged—
I may not love you—for I am engaged!

LADY SANGAZURE (horrified)
Engaged!

MR WELLS
Engaged!
To a maiden fair,
With bright brown hair,
And a sweet and simple smile,
Who waits for me
By the sounding sea,
On a South Pacific isle.
MR. W. (aside)
A lie! No maiden waits me there!

LADY SANGAZURE(mournfully)
She has bright brown hair;

MR WELLS (aside)
A lie! No maiden smiles on me!

LADY SANGAZURE (mournfully)
By the sounding sea!

ENSEMBLE

LADY SANGAZURE	**MR WELLS**
Oh agony, rage, despair!	Oh, agony, rage, despair!
The maiden has bright brown hair,	Oh, where will this end—oh, where?
And mine is as white as snow!	I should like very much to know!

False man, it will be your fault, If I go to my family vault, And bury my life-long woe!	It will certainly be my fault, If she goes to her family vault, To bury her life-long woe!

BOTH.
The family vault—the family vault.
It will certainly be (your/my) fault.
If (I go/she goes) to (my/her) family vault,
To bury (my/her) life-long woe!

(Exit LADY SANGAZURE, in great anguish, accompanied by MR WELLS)

Enter ALINE, Recitative

Alexis! Doubt me not, my loved one! See,
Thine uttered will is sovereign law to me!
All fear—all thought of ill I cast away!
It is may darling's will, and I obey!

(She drinks the philtre.)

The fearful deed is done,
My love is near!
I go to meet my own
In trembling fear!
If o'er us aught of ill
Should cast a shade,
It was my darling's will,
And I obeyed!

(As ALINE is going off, she meets DR DALY, entering pensively. He is playing on a flageolet. Under the influence of the spell she at once becomes strangely fascinated by him, and exhibits every symptom of being hopelessly in love with him.)

SONG—**DR. DALY**
Oh, my voice is sad and low
And with timid step I go—
For with load of love o'er laden
I enquire of every maiden,
"Will you wed me, little lady?
Will you share my cottage shady?"
Little lady answers "No!
Thank you for your kindly proffer—
Good your heart, and full your coffer;
Yet I must decline your offer—
I'm engaged to So-and-so!"
So-and-so!
So-and-so! (flageolet solo)

She's engaged to So-and-so!
What a rogue young hearts to pillage;
What a worker on Love's tillage!
Every maiden in the village
Is engage to So-and-so!
So-and-so!
So-and-so! (flageolet solo)
All engaged to So-and-so!

(At the end of the song DR DALY sees ALINE, and, under the influence of the potion, falls in love with her.)

ENSEMBLE—**ALINE and DR. DALY**
Oh, joyous boon! oh, mad delight;
Oh, sun and moon! oh, day and night!
Rejoice, rejoice with me!
Proclaim our joy, ye birds above—
Yet brooklets, murmur forth our love,
In choral ecstasy:

ALINE
Oh, joyous boon!

DR DALY
Oh, mad delight!

ALINE
Oh, sun and moon!

DR DALY
Oh, day and night!

BOTH
Ye birds, and brooks, and fruitful trees,
With choral joy, delight the breeze—
Rejoice, rejoice with me!

Enter ALEXIS

ALEXIS (with rapture).
Aline my only love, my happiness!
The philtre—you have tasted it?

ALINE (with confusion).
Yes! Yes!

ALEXIS
Oh, joy, mine, mine for ever, and for aye!

(Embraces her.)

ALINE
Alexis, don't do that—you must not!

(DR DALY interposes between them)

ALEXIS (amazed).
Why?

DUET—ALINE and DR. DALY

ALINE
Alas! that lovers thus should meet:
Oh, pity, pity me!
Oh, charge me not with cold deceit;
Oh, pity, pity me!
You bade me drink—with trembling awe
I drank, and, by the potion's law,
I loved the very first I saw!
Oh, pity, pity, me!

DR DALY
My dear young friend, consoled be—
We pity, pity you.
In this I'm not an agent free—
We pity, pity you.
Some most extraordinary spell
O'er us has cast its magic fell—
The consequence I need not tell.
We pity, pit you.

ENSEMBLE

Some most extraordinary spell
O'er (us/them) has cast its magic fell—
The consequence (we/they) need not tell.
(We/They) pity, pity (thee!/me).

ALEXIS (furiously)
False one, begone—I spurn thee,
To thy new lover turn thee!
Thy perfidy all men shall know,

ALINE (wildly)
I could not help it!

ALEXIS (calling off)
Come one, come all!

DR DALY
We could not help it!

ALEXIS (calling off)
Obey my call!

ALINE (wildly)
I could not help it!

ALEXIS (calling off)
Come hither, run!

DR DALY
We could not help it!

ALEXIS (calling off)
Come, every one!

Enter all the characters except LADY SANGAZURE and MR WELLS.

CHORUS
Oh, what is the matter, and what is the clatter?
He's glowering at her, and threatens a blow!
Oh, why does he batter the girl he did flatter?
And why does the latter recoil from him so?

RECITATIVE—**ALEXIS**
Prepare for sad surprises—
My love Aline despises!
No thought of sorrow shames her—
Another lover claims her!
Be his, false girl, for better or for worse—
But, ere you leave me, may a lover's curse—

DR DALY (coming forward)
Hold! Be just. This poor child drank the philtre at your instance. She hurried off to meet you—but, most unhappily, she met me instead. As you had administered the potion to both of us, the result was inevitable. But fear nothing from me—I will be no man's rival. I shall quit the country at once—and bury my sorrow in the congenial gloom of a Colonial Bishopric.

ALEXIS
My excellent old friend!

(Taking his hand—then turning to MR WELLS, who has entered with LADY SANGAZURE)

Oh, Mr. Wells, what, what is to be done?

MR WELLS
I do not know—and yet—there is one means by which this spell may be removed.

ALEXIS
Name it—oh, name it!

MR WELLS
Or you or I must yield up his life to Ahrimanes. I would rather it were you. I should have no hesitation in sacrificing my own life to spare yours, but we take stock next week, and it would not be fair on the Co.

ALEXIS
True. Well, I am ready!

ALINE
No, no—Alexis—it must not be! Mr. Wells, if he must die that all may be restored to their old loves, what is to become of me? I should be left out in the cold, with no love to be restored to!

MR WELLS
True—I did not think of that. (To the others) My friends, I appeal to you, and I will leave the decision in your hands.

FINALE

MR WELLS
Or I or he
Must die!
Which shall it be?
Reply!

SIR MARMADUKE
Die thou!
Thou art the cause of all offending!

DR DALY
Die thou!
Yield to this decree unbending!

ALL
Die thou!

MR WELLS
So be it! I submit! My fate is sealed.
To public execration thus I yield!

(Falls on trap)

Be happy all—leave me to my despair—
I go—it matters not with whom—or where!

(Gong)

(All quit their present partners, and rejoin their old lovers.

SIR MARMADUKE leaves MRS PARTLET, and goes to LADY SANGAZURE.

ALINE leaves DR DALY, and goes to ALEXIS. DR DALY leaves ALINE, and goes to CONSTANCE. NOTARY
leaves CONSTANCE, and goes to MRS PARTLET.

All
the Chorus makes a corresponding change.)

ALL

GENTLEMEN
Oh, my adored one!

LADIES
Unmingled joy!

GENTLEMEN
Ecstatic rapture!

LADIES
Beloved boy!

(They embrace)

SIR MARMADUKE
Come to my mansion, all of you! At least
We'll crown our rapture with another feast!

ENSEMBLE

SIR MARMADUKE, LADY SANGAZURE, ALEXIS, and ALINE
Now to the banquet we press—
Now for the eggs and the ham—
Now for the mustard and cress—
Now for the strawberry jam!

CHORUS
Now to the banquet, etc.

DR. DALY, CONSTANCE, NOTARY, and MRS. PARTLET
Now for the tea of our host—

Now for the rollicking bun—
Now for the muffin and toast—
Now for the gay Sally Lunn!

CHORUS.
Now for the tea, etc.

(General Dance)

(During the symphony MR WELLS sinks through the trap, amid red fire.)

CURTAIN

W.S. Gilbert – A Short Biography

Sir William Schwenck Gilbert was born on November 18th, 1836 at 17 Southampton Street, Strand, London. His father, also named William, was a naval surgeon, who later became a writer of novels and short stories, some of which were illustrated by his son. Gilbert's mother was the former Anne Mary Bye Morris (1812–1888), the daughter of Thomas Morris, an apothecary.

Gilbert's parents were distant and stern, and there was no close bond between either themselves or their children (the marriage was to eventually break up in 1876). Gilbert had three younger sisters, Jane Morris, Anne Maude Mary Florence.

As a child, Gilbert was nicknamed "Bab".

The family travelled to Italy in 1838 and then France before finally returning to settle in London in 1847.

Gilbert was educated in Boulogne, France from age seven, then at Western Grammar School, Brompton, London, before the Great Ealing School, where he became head boy and wrote plays for school performances. He then attended King's College London, graduating in 1856.

His first thought for a career was to take examinations for a commission in the Royal Artillery, but the Crimean War had just ended and with fewer recruits needed only a commission in a line regiment was available. He opted instead for the Civil Service and was an assistant clerk in the Privy Council Office for four years. He hated it. In 1859 he joined the Militia, a part-time volunteer force, and served until 1878, as his other work allowed, and reached the rank of Captain.

To supplement his income Gilbert wrote a variety of stories, comic rants, theatre reviews (many in the form of a parody of the play being reviewed), and, using the pseudonym of his childhood nickname, "Bab" illustrated poems for several comic magazines, primarily Fun, started in 1861. His work was also published in the Cornhill Magazine, London Society, Tinsley's Magazine and Temple Bar. Gilbert was also the London correspondent for L'Invalide Russe and a drama critic for the Illustrated London Times. In the 1860s he also contributed to Tom Hood's Christmas annuals, to Saturday Night, the Comic News and the Savage Club Papers.

The poems, illustrated humorously by Gilbert, proved immensely popular and were reprinted in book form as the Bab Ballads. He would later return to many of these as source material for his plays and comic operas.

In 1863 he received a bequest of £300 allowing him to leave the civil service and attempt a career as a barrister. Unfortunately, he managed to attract few clients.

However, these events happily coincided with his first professionally produced play; Uncle Baby, which ran for seven weeks in the autumn of 1863.

In 1865–66, Gilbert collaborated with Charles Millward on several pantomimes, including Hush-a-Bye, Baby, On the Tree Top, or, Harlequin Fortunia, King Frog of Frog Island, and the Magic Toys of Lowther Arcade (1866).

Gilbert's first solo success, however, came a few days after Hush-a-Bye Baby premiered. His friend and mentor, Tom Robertson, was asked to deliver a pantomime within two weeks. Robertson couldn't and recommended Gilbert who took the job. Written and rushed to the stage in 10 days, Dulcamara, or the Little Duck and the Great Quack, a burlesque of Gaetano Donizetti's L'elisir d'amore, proved very popular. This led to a long series of further Gilbert opera burlesques, pantomimes and farces, full of dreadful puns, but showing signs of the satire that would later be such an integral part of Gilbert's work.

After a failed relationship with the novelist Annie Thomas, Gilbert married Lucy Agnes Turner, whom he affectionately called "Kitty", in 1867; she was 11 years his junior. They were socially active both in London and later at their new home at Grim's Dyke, often holding dinner parties. Although they had no children they had many pets, including several exotic ones.

Next followed Gilbert's biggest success so far; his penultimate operatic parody, Robert the Devil, a burlesque of Giacomo Meyerbeer's opera, Robert le diable, part of a triple bill that opened the Gaiety Theatre, London in 1868. It ran for over 100 nights.

In Victorian theatre, Gilbert's burlesques were considered very tasteful compared to the offerings of others. He would now move away from burlesque to plays with original plots and fewer puns. His first was An Old Score in 1869.

Theatre, at this time had fallen into disrepute. London was awash with poorly translated French operettas and cheaply written, prurient Victorian burlesques. From 1869 to 1875, Gilbert joined with Thomas German Reed (and his wife Priscilla), whose Gallery of Illustration sought to regain some of theatre's lost respect with family entertainments. This would be so successful that by 1885 Gilbert could safely state that original British plays were appropriate for an innocent 15-year-old girl to watch.

The initial work for the Gallery of Illustration, No Cards, was the first of six musical entertainments for the German Reeds, by Gilbert some with music composed by Thomas German Reed.

The German Reeds' intimate theatre allowed Gilbert to develop a personal style that would also cede to him control all aspects of production; set, costumes, direction and stage management.

Gilbert's first big hit at the Gallery of Illustration, Ages Ago, also opened in 1869. It marked the beginning of a collaboration with the composer Frederic Clay that would last seven years and cover four works. It was at a rehearsal for Ages Ago that Clay introduced Gilbert to Arthur Sullivan.

These musical works gave Gilbert a valuable education as a lyricist and he perfected the 'topsy-turvy' style that he had been developing in his Bab Ballads, where the humour was derived by setting up a ridiculous premise and following through on its logical consequences, however absurd they might be.

Ever busy he found time to create several 'fairy comedies' at the Haymarket Theatre. The premise was the idea of self-revelation by characters under the influence of magic or some supernatural experience. The first was The Palace of Truth (1870), based partly on a story by Madame de Genlis. In 1871, with Pygmalion and Galatea, one of seven plays that he produced that year, Gilbert scored his greatest hit to date. Together, these plays including The Wicked World (1873), Sweethearts (1874), and Broken Hearts (1875), did for Gilbert on the dramatic stage what the German Reed entertainments had done for him on the musical stage: they established that his talents were large and burgeoning, a writer of wide range, as comfortable with human drama as much as farcical humour.

Contemptorous with this period Gilbert pushed the satirical boundaries. He collaborated with Gilbert Arthur à Beckett on The Happy Land (1873), in part, a parody of his own The Wicked World, which was briefly banned because of its caricatures of Gladstone and his ministers. Similarly, The Realm of Joy (1873) was set in the lobby of a theatre performing a scandalous play (implied to be the Happy Land), with many jokes at the expense of the Lord Chamberlain (the "Lord High Disinfectant", as he's referred to in the play). In Charity (1874), however, Gilbert uses the freedom of the stage in a different way: to illuminate the contrasting ways in which society treated men and women who had sex outside of marriage. It was ground breaking and some see it as anticipating the 'problem plays' of Shaw and Ibsen.

Once established as a writer Gilbert was also the stage director, with strong, forceful opinions on how they should best be performed.

In Gilbert's 1874 burlesque, Rosencrantz and Guildenstern, the character Hamlet, in his speech to the players, sums up Gilbert's theory of comic acting: "I hold that there is no such antick fellow as your bombastical hero who doth so earnestly spout forth his folly as to make his hearers believe that he is unconscious of all incongruity". Again some say with this he prepared the ground for playwrights such as George Bernard Shaw and Oscar Wilde to be able to flourish.

Tom Robertson had "introduced Gilbert both to the revolutionary notion of disciplined rehearsals and to mise-en-scène or unity of style in the whole presentation – direction, design, music, acting." Like Robertson, Gilbert demanded discipline in his actors, that they know their lines, enunciate them clearly and keep to his stage directions, a new development for actors at the time. It also ushered in the replacement of the star with the disciplined ensemble.

Gilbert was meticulous in his preparations, making models of the stage and designing every action in advance. He refused to work with actors who challenged him. He was famous for demonstrating the action himself, even as he grew older. Such was his interest in standards that even during long runs and revivals, he closely supervised the performances of his plays, making sure that no one made additions or deletions.

Sir Arthur Seymour Sullivan, MVO was born on May 13th 1842 in Lambeth, London. His father, Thomas Sullivan, a military bandmaster, clarinetist and music teacher, was born in Ireland and raised in Chelsea, London, and his mother, Mary Clementina (née Coghlan, English born, of Irish and Italian descent. Thomas Sullivan was based from 1845 to 1857 at the Royal Military College, Sandhurst, where he was the bandmaster and taught music privately to supplement his income. Young Sullivan became proficient with many of the instruments in the band and had composed an anthem, "By the waters of Babylon", by the age of eight. While proudly observing his son's obvious musical talent, he knew, at first hand, how insecure a profession it was and discouraged him from pursuing it.

Three years later whilst at a private school in Bayswater, Sullivan persuaded his parents and headmaster to allow him to apply for membership in the choir of the Chapel Royal. There were concerns that Sullivan at nearly 12 years of age was too old to be a treble as his voice would soon break. But he was accepted and soon became a soloist and, by 1856, was promoted to "first boy". Troublingly, even at this age, Sullivan's health was delicate, and he was easily fatigued.

However, Sullivan flourished under the training of the Reverend Thomas Helmore, and began to compose anthems and songs. Helmore arranged for one pieces, "O Israel", to be published in 1855.

In 1856, the Royal Academy of Music awarded the first Mendelssohn Scholarship to the 14-year-old Sullivan, granting him a year's training at the academy. His principal teacher there was John Goss, whose own teacher had been a pupil of Mozart. Initially Sullivan studied piano.

Sullivan's scholarship was extended to a second year, and then a third so that he could study in Germany, at the Leipzig Conservatoire. There he was trained in Mendelssohn's ideas and techniques as well as being exposed to Schubert, Verdi, Bach, and Wagner. Sullivan was an eager pupil and always looking for inspiration. On a visit to a synagogue, he was so struck by some of the cadences and progressions in the music that three decades later he would recall them for use in his serious opera, Ivanhoe.

Though the scholarship in Leipzig, was for one year he stayed for three. Sullivan credited his Leipzig period with rapid and sustained musical growth. His graduation piece, in 1861, was a set of incidental music to Shakespeare's The Tempest. Revised and expanded, it was performed at the Crystal Palace in 1862, a year after his return to London. It was an immediate sensation. He began building a reputation as England's most promising young composer.

He now embarked on composing with a series of ambitious works, interspersed with hymns, parlour songs and other light pieces of a more commercial nature. These compositions could not support him financially, and from 1861 to 1872 he supplemented his income working as a church organist, a task he enjoyed, and as a music teacher, sometimes at the Crystal Palace School, which he hated and gave up as soon as his finances allowed. Sullivan also took an early chance to compose pieces for royalty with the wedding of the Prince of Wales in 1863.

Sullivan began to put voice and orchestra together with The Masque at Kenilworth (Birmingham Festival, 1864). For Covent Garden that same year he composed his first ballet, L'Île Enchantée.

1865 saw Sullivan initiated into Freemasonry and was Grand Organist of the United Grand Lodge of England in 1887 during Queen Victoria's Golden Jubilee.

In 1866, he premiered his Irish Symphony and Cello Concerto, his only works in these genres. In the same year, his Overture in C (In Memoriam), commemorating the recent death of his father, was a commission from the Norwich Festival.

His overture Marmion was premiered by the Philharmonic Society in 1867. The Times called it "another step in advance on the part of the only composer of any remarkable promise that just at present we can boast."

Sadly, his initial attempt at opera, The Sapphire Necklace (1863–64) with a libretto by Henry F. Chorley, was not produced and, apart from the Overture and two songs published separately, is now lost.

His first surviving opera, Cox and Box (1866), was written for a private performance. It then received charity performances in London and Manchester, and was later produced at the Gallery of Illustration, where it ran for an extraordinary 264 performances. His soon to be partner, W. S. Gilbert, writing in Fun magazine, announced the score as superior to F. C. Burnand's libretto.

In 1867 Sullivan and Burnand were commissioned by Thomas German Reed for a two-act opera, The Contrabandista (revised and expanded as The Chieftain in 1894), but it was a much more modest success.

Sullivan wrote a group of seven part songs in 1868, the best-known of which is "The Long Day Closes". His last major work of the 1860s was a short oratorio, The Prodigal Son, which premiered in Worcester Cathedral as part of the 1869 Three Choirs Festival to much praise.

The Overture di Ballo, Sullivan's most enduring work, was composed for the Birmingham Festival in 1870.

1871 was a busy year. Sullivan published his only song cycle, The Window; or, The Songs of the Wrens, to words by Tennyson, and wrote the first of a series of suites of incidental music for West End productions of Shakespeare plays. Later in the year he composed a dramatic cantata, On Shore and Sea, for the opening of the London International Exhibition, and the beautiful hymn Onward, Christian Soldiers, with words by Sabine Baring-Gould. The Salvation Army adopted it and it has become one of Britain's best loved hymns.

Gilbert & Sullivan – The Collaboration Begins

In 1871, John Hollingshead commissioned Gilbert to work with Sullivan on a holiday piece for Christmas, entitled Thespis, or The Gods Grown Old, at the Gaiety Theatre. It was a success and its run was extended beyond the length of the Gaiety's normal run. And that seemed to be that.

Gilbert and Sullivan now went their separate ways. Gilbert worked again with Clay on Happy Arcadia (1872), and with Alfred Cellier on Topsyturveydom (1874), as well as several farces, operetta libretti, extravaganzas, fairy comedies, adaptations from novels, translations from the French. In 1874, he published his last piece for Fun magazine ("Rosencrantz and Guildenstern"), almost three years after his last and then promptly resigned citing disapproval of the new owner's other publishing interests.

Sullivan was busy on large-scale works in the early 1870s with the Festival Te Deum (Crystal Palace, 1872); and the oratorio, The Light of the World (Birmingham Festival, 1873). He also wrote suites of incidental music for productions of The Merry Wives of Windsor at the Gaiety in 1874 and Henry VIII at the Theatre Royal, Manchester in 1877 as well as continuing composing hymns.

In 1873, Sullivan had also contributed songs to Burnand's Christmas "drawing room extravaganza", The Miller and His Man.

By 1875 conditions were right for Gilbert and Sullivan to work together again. Back in 1868, Gilbert had published a short comedic libretto in Fun magazine entitled "Trial by Jury: An Operetta". In 1873, Gilbert had arranged with theatrical manager and composer, Carl Rosa, to expand this work into a one-act libretto. It was arranged that Rosa's wife was to sing the role of the plaintiff. Tragically, Rosa's wife died in childbirth in 1874. Gilbert offered the libretto to Richard D'Oyly Carte, but Carte could not use the piece at that time.

The project seemed grounded. A few months later Carte, was managing the Royalty Theatre, needed a short piece to pair with Offenbach's La Périchole. Carte had previously conducted Sullivan's Cox and Box and remembering that Gilbert had suggested a libretto to him, he reunited Gilbert and Sullivan. The result was the one-act comic opera Trial by Jury. Starring Sullivan's brother Fred as the Learned Judge, it became a surprise hit, as well as earning lavish praise from the critics. It played for over 300 performances in its first few seasons.

A short time after Trial had opened Sullivan wrote The Zoo, another one-act comic opera, with a libretto by B. C. Stephenson. It did not perform well. Now the path was clear for Gilbert & Sullivan to reteam together in earnest and dominate light opera for the next 15 years.

Light opera was not considered of much worth by serious critics. Gilbert wanted greater respect for himself and his profession. At that time plays were not published in a form suitable for a "gentleman's library", they were in the main cheap and unattractive in their look designed mainly for use by actors rather than the home reader. Gilbert now arranged in late 1875 for the publishers Chatto and Windus to print a volume of his plays in a format designed to appeal to the general reader, with an attractive binding and clear type, containing Gilbert's most respectable plays, including his most serious works, and mischievously capped off with Trial by Jury.

After the success of Trial by Jury, there were discussions towards reviving Thespis, but Gilbert and Sullivan were not able to agree on terms with Carte and his backers. The score to Thespis was never published, and tragically most of the music is now lost.

Carte took some time to gather together funds for another opera, and in this gap the ever-busy Gilbert produced several works including Tom Cobb (1875), Eyes and No Eyes (1875), and Princess Toto (1876), his last and most ambitious work with Clay, a three-act comic opera with full orchestra. He also found time to write two serious works, Broken Hearts (1875) and Dan'l Druce, Blacksmith (1876) and his most successful comic play, Engaged (1877), which inspired Oscar Wilde's The Importance of Being Earnest.

It was only by 1877 that Carte finally assembled enough investors to form the Comedy Opera Company with a mandate to launch a series of original English comic operas, beginning with a third collaboration between Gilbert and Sullivan, The Sorcerer, in November 1877.

The Sorcerer (1877), ran for 178 performances, a success by the standards of the day, but H.M.S. Pinafore (1878), which followed it, turned Gilbert and Sullivan into an international phenomenon. The bright and cheerful music of Pinafore was composed during a time when Sullivan was in the middle of a health scare. He was in terrible pain from a kidney stone. H.M.S. Pinafore ran for 571 performances in London, the then-second-longest theatrical run in history, it also gave birth to and more than 150 unauthorised productions in America alone. Although this increased the reach of their reputations it added nothing to their profits.

It was noted in the Times review of H.M.S. Pinafore that the opera was an early attempt at the establishment of a "national musical stage" ... free from risqué French "improprieties" and without the "aid" of Italian and German musical models.

As the profits rolled in came acrimony among the investors who felt the shares were unequal. One night the other Comedy Opera Company partners hired thugs to storm the theatre to steal the sets and costumes in order that they could mount a rival production. This was beaten off by stagehands and others at the theatre loyal to Carte. Carte was to now continue as sole impresario of the newly renamed D'Oyly Carte Opera Company.

For the next decade, the Savoy Operas were Gilbert's principal activity. The successful comic operas with Sullivan continued to appear every year or two, several of them being among the longest-running productions of the musical stage. After Pinafore came The Pirates of Penzance (1879), Patience (1881), Iolanthe (1882), Princess Ida (1884 and based on Gilbert's earlier farce, The Princess), The Mikado (1885), Ruddigore (1887), The Yeomen of the Guard (1888), and The Gondoliers (1889). Gilbert not only directed and oversaw all aspects of production, but he designed the costumes himself for Patience, Iolanthe, Princess Ida, and Ruddigore. He insisted on precise and authentic sets and costumes, which provided a foundation to ground and focus his absurd characters and situations.

In 1878, Gilbert realised a lifelong dream to play Harlequin, which he did at the Gaiety Theatre in an amateur charity production of The Forty Thieves, written partly by himself. Gilbert trained for Harlequin's stylised dancing with his friend John D'Auban, who had arranged the dances for some of his plays and would choreograph most of the Gilbert and Sullivan operas. Producer John Hollingshead later remembered, "the gem of the performance was the grimly earnest and determined Harlequin of W. S. Gilbert. It gave me an idea of what Oliver Cromwell would have made of the character."

In 1879, Sullivan suggested to a reporter from The New York Times the secret of his success with Gilbert: "His ideas are as suggestive for music as they are quaint and laughable. His numbers ... always give me musical ideas."

During this time, Gilbert and Sullivan also collaborated on one other major work. In 1880, Sullivan was appointed director of the triennial Leeds Music Festival. For his first festival he was commissioned to write a sacred choral work. He chose Henry Hart Milman's 1822 dramatic poem based on the life and death of Saint Margaret the Virgin for its basis. It premiered at the Leeds music festival in October 1880. Gilbert arranged the original epic poem by Henry Hart Milman into a libretto suitable for the music.

Carte opened the next Gilbert and Sullivan piece, Patience, in April 1881 at London's Opera Comique, where their past three operas had played. In October, Patience transferred to the new, larger, state-of-the-art (it was the first theatre to be lit entirely with electricity) Savoy Theatre, built with the profits of the previous Gilbert and Sullivan works.

From now on all of the partnership's collaborations were produced at the Savoy. The first to actually premiere here was Iolanthe in 1882, it was their fourth hit in a row.

Cracks were beginning to surface between the partners. Sullivan, despite the financial security, began to view his work with Gilbert as beneath his skills, as well as being repetitious. After Iolanthe, Sullivan had not intended to write a new work with Gilbert, but when his broker went bankrupt in late 1882 he suffered serious financial loss. Needs must and Sullivan buckled down to continue writing Savoy operas. In February 1883, he and Gilbert signed a five-year agreement with Carte, requiring them to produce a new comic opera on six months' notice.

The ever watchful Gilbert had the previous year installed a telephone in his home and another at the prompt desk at the Savoy Theatre, so that he could listen in on performances and rehearsals from his home study. Gilbert had referred to the new technology in Pinafore in 1878, only two years after the device was invented and before London even had telephones.

Better news arrived for Sullivan on May 22nd, 1883, when he was knighted by Queen Victoria for his "services ... rendered to the promotion of the art of music" in Britain. The musical establishment, and many critics, believed that this would put an end to his career as a composer of comic opera – that a musical knight should not stoop below oratorio or grand opera. But Sullivan having just signed the five-year agreement and the financial security that gave him could no nothing to change course now.

The next opera, Princess Ida in 1884, which was the duo's only three-act, blank verse work, stuttered. Its run was much shorter. Sullivan's score was praised but with box office receipts lagging in March 1884, Carte gave the six months' notice, under the partnership contract, requiring a new opera.

Sullivan's friend, composer Frederic Clay, had suffered a serious stroke in early December 1883 that ended his career at only 45 years of age. Sullivan, with his own longstanding kidney problems, and his desire to devote himself to more serious music, replied to Carte, "It is impossible for me to do another piece of the character of those already written by Gilbert and myself."

Gilbert however was already at work on it. His idea revolved around a plot in which people fell in love against their wills after taking a magic lozenge. Sullivan was unequoviacal in his response. On April 1st, 1884 he wrote that he had "come to the end of my tether with the operas. I have been continually keeping down the music in order that not one syllable should be lost.... I should like to set a story of human interest & probability where the humorous words would come in a humorous not serious situation, & where, if the situation were a tender or dramatic one the words would be of similar character."

There was now a lengthy exchange of correspondence in which Sullivan called Gilbert's plot sketch (particularly the "lozenge" element) unacceptably mechanical, and too similar in both its grotesque "elements of topsyturveydom" and in actual plot to their earlier work, especially The Sorcerer, and requested, time and again, that a new subject be found.

This impasse was finally resolved on May 8th when Gilbert proposed a plot that would be their most successful: The Mikado (1885). It was to run for a staggering 672 performances.

In 1886, Sullivan composed his last large-scale choral work of the decade. It was a cantata for the Leeds Festival, The Golden Legend, based on Longfellow's poem of the same name. Apart from the comic operas, this proved to be Sullivan's best received full-length work. It was given hundreds of performances during his lifetime alone.

Ruddigore followed The Mikado in 1887. It was profitable, but its nine-month run was deemed to be disappointing compared with the earlier Savoy operas.

Gilbert was always keen to use a good idea again and proposed for their next piece another version of the magic lozenge plot. It was immediately rejected by Sullivan. Gilbert finally proposed a quite serious opera, to which Sullivan was in agreement. Although not a grand opera, The Yeomen of the Guard (1888) gave him the opportunity to compose his most ambitious stage work to date. In 1885, Sullivan had told an interviewer, ""The opera of the future is a compromise (among the French, German and Italian schools) – a sort of eclectic school, a selection of the merits of each one. I myself will make an attempt to produce a grand opera of this new school. ... Yes, it will be an historical work, and it is the dream of my life."

After The Yeomen of the Guard opened, Sullivan turned once again to Shakespeare and composed incidental music for Henry Irving's production of Macbeth (1888).

Sullivan wished to produce further serious works with Gilbert. He had collaborated with no other librettist since 1875. Gilbert felt the reaction to The Yeomen of the Guard had "not been so convincing as to warrant us in assuming that the public want something more earnest still." Gilbert countered by proposing that Sullivan should go ahead with his plan to write a grand opera, as well as comic works for the Savoy. Sullivan was not immediately persuaded. He replied, "I have lost the liking for writing comic opera, and entertain very grave doubts as to my power of doing it."

Nevertheless, Sullivan soon commissioned a grand opera libretto from Julian Sturgis (the recommendation came from Gilbert), while suggesting to Gilbert that he revive an old idea for an opera set in colourful Venice. The comic opera was completed first in 1889. The Gondoliers has been described as a pinnacle of Sullivan's achievement. It was to be the last great Gilbert and Sullivan success.

In April 1890, during the run of The Gondoliers, Gilbert objected to Carte's financial accounts which included a charge to the partnership for the cost of new carpeting for the Savoy Theatre lobby. Gilbert believed that this was a maintenance expense that should be charged to Carte alone. Carte who was building a new theatre to present Sullivan's forthcoming grand opera was adamant that it was legitimate. Sullivan sided with Carte, even going so far as to testify erroneously as to certain old debts.

The partners were in fundamental disagreement and the relationship was for all intents and purposes ruptured.

Gilbert took legal action against Carte and Sullivan and refused to write a word more for the Savoy. Sullivan wrote to Gilbert in September 1890 that he was "physically and mentally ill over this wretched business. I have not yet got over the shock of seeing our names coupled ... in hostile antagonism over a few miserable pounds".

From Gilbert's point of view Carte had either made a series of serious blunders in the accounts, or deliberately attempted to swindle his partners.

Gilbert wrote to Sullivan on May 28th, 1891, a year after the end of the "Quarrel", that Carte had admitted "an unintentional overcharge of nearly £1,000 in the electric lighting accounts alone." It seemed to illustrate Gilbert's point.

Work beckoned for Gilbert and he got on with it. He wrote The Mountebanks with Alfred Cellier and then a flop Haste to the Wedding with George Grossmith. Sullivan wrote Haddon Hall with Sydney Grundy.

In the Courts Gilbert prevailed in the lawsuit and felt vindicated. Although there was acrimony and bitterness between them the partnership had been so profitable that, after the financial failure of the Royal English Opera House, Carte and his wife sought to reunite the author and composer.

In 1891, after numerous failed attempts at a reconciliation, Tom Chappell, the music publisher who printed the Gilbert and Sullivan operas, stepped in to mediate between his two most profitable artists, and within two weeks, against the odds, had succeeded. The result was to be two more operas: Utopia, Limited (1893) and The Grand Duke (1896).

A third was almost achieved when Gilbert offered a third libretto to Sullivan (His Excellency, 1894), but his insistence on casting Nancy McIntosh, his protegée from Utopia, led to Sullivan's refusal.

Utopia, was only a modest success, and The Grand Duke, in which a theatrical troupe, by means of a "statutory duel" and a conspiracy, takes political control of a grand duchy, was a failure.

The partnership now ended for good.

Graciously Gilbert would late write, "... Savoy opera was snuffed out by the deplorable death of my distinguished collaborator, Sir Arthur Sullivan. When that event occurred, I saw no one with whom I felt that I could work with satisfaction and success, and so I discontinued to write libretti."

WS Gilbert – Life After the Partnership

In 1889 Gilbert financed the building of the Garrick Theatre. The following year the Gilberts moved to Grim's Dyke in Harrow. In 1891, Gilbert was appointed Justice of the Peace for Middlesex. After casting Nancy McIntosh in Utopia, Limited, he and Lady Gilbert developed an affection for her, and she eventually gained the status of an unofficially adopted daughter, moving to Grim's Dyke to live with them. She continued living there, even after Gilbert's death, until Lady Gilbert's death in 1936.

Although Gilbert announced a retirement from the theatre after the poor initial run of his last work with Sullivan, The Grand Duke (1896) and the poor reception of his 1897 play The Fortune Hunter, he produced at least three more plays over the last dozen years of his life, including an unsuccessful opera, Fallen Fairies (1909), with Edward German.

Gilbert, as we know was very keen on keeping his plays in the shape they were originally intended and continued to supervise the various revivals of his works by the D'Oyly Carte Opera Company, including its London Repertory seasons in 1906–09.

The last play he wrote, The Hooligan, produced just four months before his death, is a study of a young condemned thug in a prison cell. Gilbert shows sympathy for his protagonist, the son of a thief who, brought up among thieves, kills his girlfriend.

This grim, yet powerful piece, became one of Gilbert's most successful serious dramas, and it is easy to see why many thought he was developing a new style only for death to rob of us of what would surely be a fascinating journey.

In these last years, Gilbert wrote children's book versions of H.M.S. Pinafore and The Mikado giving, in some cases, backstory that is not found in the librettos.

Official recognition for him came on July 15th, 1907 with his knighthood in recognition of his contributions to drama. Gilbert was the first British writer ever to receive a knighthood for his plays alone—earlier dramatist knights were knighted for political and other services.

On May 29th, 1911, Gilbert was about to give a swimming lesson to Winifred Isabel Emery and 17-year-old Ruby Preece in the lake of his home, Grim's Dyke, when Preece lost her footing and called for help. Gilbert dived in to save her but suffered a heart attack in the middle of the lake and died.

William Schwenck was cremated at Golders Green and his ashes buried at the Church of St. John the Evangelist, Stanmore. The inscription on Gilbert's memorial on the south wall of the Thames Embankment in London reads: "His Foe was Folly, and his Weapon Wit".

George Grossmith wrote to The Daily Telegraph that, although Gilbert had been described as an autocrat at rehearsals, "That was really only his manner when he was playing the part of stage director at rehearsals. As a matter of fact, he was a generous, kind true gentleman, and I use the word in the purest and original sense."

Gilbert's legacy, aside from building the Garrick Theatre are the canon of Savoy Operas and other works that are either still being performed or in print all these years later. He has made a lasting and defining influence on both the American and British musical theatre. The innovations in content and form of the works that he and Sullivan developed, and in Gilbert's theories of acting and stage direction, directly influenced the development of the modern musical throughout the 20th century. Gilbert's lyrics use punning, as well as complex internal and two and three-syllable rhyme schemes, and served as a model for such 20th century Broadway lyricists as P.G. Wodehouse, Cole Porter, Ira Gershwin, and Lorenz Hart.

Gilbert's influence on the English language has also been marked, with well-known phrases such as "A policeman's lot is not a happy one", "short, sharp shock", "What never? Well, hardly ever!", and "let the punishment fit the crime" arising from his pen.

Sullivan's only grand opera, Ivanhoe, based on Walter Scott's novel, opened at Carte's new Royal English Opera House on January 31st, 1891. Sullivan completed the score too late to meet Carte's planned production date, and costs had overrun to such an extent that Carte insisted on a contractual penalty of £3,000 for the delay. However, when it opened it ran 155 consecutive performances, a wonderful run for a serious opera, and garnered good reviews. Afterwards, Carte was unable to fill the new opera house with other productions, and, unfairly, Ivanhoe was blamed for the failure of the opera house.

Later in 1891, New York beckoned for Sullivan and his music for Tennyson's The Foresters, which ran at Daly's Theatre in New York in 1892, but failed in London the following year.

Sullivan returned to comic opera, but needed a new collaborator. His next piece was Haddon Hall in 1892, with a libretto by Sydney Grundy based somewhat loosely on the elopement of Dorothy Vernon with John Manners. Although still comic, the tone and style of the work was more serious and romantic than the operas with Gilbert. It nonetheless enjoyed a run of 204 performances, and earned critical praise.

In 1894 Sullivan teamed up again with F. C. Burnand for The Chieftain, a heavily-reworked version of their earlier two-act opera, The Contrabandista, alas it failed.

The following year Sullivan provided incidental music for the Lyceum, this time for J. Comyns Carr's King Arthur.

As we know Gilbert and Sullivan did reunite for The Grand Duke in 1896. But it failed and they never worked together again. This did not affect the constant revival of their earlier operas at the Savoy.

In May 1897, Sullivan's full-length ballet, Victoria and Merrie England, opened at the Alhambra Theatre in celebration of the Queen's Diamond Jubilee. The work's seven scenes celebrate English history and culture, with the Victorian period as the grand finale. It ran for six months which was a great achievement. Following this was The Beauty Stone in 1898, with a libretto by Arthur Wing Pinero and J. Comyns Carr. Based on mediaeval morality plays the opera was a critical failure and, on the whole, a commercial failure running for only seven weeks.

Success came in 1899, to benefit "the wives and children of soldiers and sailors" on active service in the Boer War, when Sullivan composed the music of a jingoistic song, "The Absent-Minded Beggar", to a text by Rudyard Kipling. It was a sensation and raised a staggering £250,000 from performances and the sale of sheet music and other merchandise. Later that year he returned to his comic roots with In The Rose of Persia, with a libretto by Basil Hood overlapping a setting of exotic Arabian Nights with plot elements of The Mikado. It was well received, and, apart from those with Gilbert, was his most successful full-length collaboration. Another opera with Hood, The Emerald Isle, quickly went into preparation, but sadly Sullivan died before it completion.

On November 22nd, 1900 Arthur Seymour Sullivan died of heart failure, following an attack of bronchitis, at his flat in London. The unfinished opera, The Emerald Isle, was completed by Edward German and premiered in 1901. His Te Deum Laudamus, written to commemorate the end of the Boer War, was performed posthumously.

Sullivan wished to be buried in Brompton Cemetery with his parents and brother, but by order of the Queen he was buried in St. Paul's Cathedral. In addition to his knighthood, honours awarded to Sullivan in his lifetime included Doctor in Music, honoris causa, by the universities of Cambridge (1876) and Oxford (1879); Chevalier, Légion d'honneur, France (1878); The Order of the Medjidieh conferred by the Sultan of Turkey (1888); and appointment as a Member of the Fourth Class of the Royal Victorian Order (MVO) in 1897.

In all, Sullivan's artistic output included 23 operas, 13 major orchestral works, eight choral works and oratorios, two ballets, one song cycle, incidental music to several plays, numerous hymns and other church pieces, and a large body of songs, parlour ballads, part songs, carols, and piano and chamber pieces.

Although Sullivan had several long term affairs and was also known to have a roving eye that led him to frequent liaisons with many other women he never married.

Rachel Scott Russell was the first of his great loves. Her parents' disapproval meant they met secretly but by 1868, Sullivan was enmeshed in a simultaneous and secret affair with Rachel's sister Louise. Both relationships had ceased by early 1869.

Sullivan's affair with the American socialite, Fanny Ronalds, a woman three years his senior, who had two children began when they met in Paris around 1867. The affair began in earnest soon after she moved to London in 1871. Despite his wandering ways she was a constant companion up to the time of Sullivan's death, but around 1889 or 1890, the sexual relationship seems to have ended.

In 1896, the 54-year-old Sullivan proposed marriage to 22-year-old Violet Beddington but she refused.

The favourite playgrounds for Sullivan were Paris and the south of France, with friends ranging from European royalty to Claude Debussy, and where the casinos enabled him to indulge his passion for gambling.

Sullivan enjoyed playing tennis although, according to George Grossmith, "I have seen some bad lawn-tennis players in my time, but I never saw anyone so bad as Arthur Sullivan".

He was devoted to his parents, particularly his mother, until her death in 1882. Henry Lytton wrote, "I believe there was never a more affectionate tie than that which existed between Sullivan and his mother, a very witty old lady, and one who took an exceptional pride in her son's accomplishments.

Sullivan once explained his method of working; "I don't use the piano in composition – that would limit me terribly". Sullivan explained that he did not wait for inspiration, but had "to dig for it. ... I decide on the rhythm before I come to the question of melody. ... I mark out the metre in dots and dashes, and not until I have quite settled on the rhythm do I proceed to actual notation."

In composing the Savoy operas, Sullivan wrote the vocal lines of the musical numbers first, and these were given to the actors. He, or an assistant, improvised a piano accompaniment at the early rehearsals; he wrote the orchestrations later, after he had seen what Gilbert's stage business would be. He left the overtures until last and often delegated their composition, based on his outlines, to his assistants, often adding his suggestions or corrections. Those Sullivan wrote himself include Thespis, Iolanthe, Princess Ida, The Yeomen of the Guard, The Gondoliers, The Grand Duke and probably Utopia Limited. Most of the overtures are structured as a potpourri of tunes from the operas in three sections: fast, slow and fast. The overtures from the Gilbert and Sullivan operas remain popular. Sullivan invariably conducted the operas on their opening nights.

In general, Sullivan preferred to write in major keys. In the Savoy operas less than 5% of the numbers are in a minor key and even in his serious works the major prevails. Sullivan was happy on occasion to use chords traditionally considered technically incorrect. When reproached for using consecutive fifths in Cox and Box, he replied "if 5ths turn up it doesn't matter, so long as there is no offence to the ear."

Sullivan's orchestra for the Savoy Operas was typical of any other pit orchestra of his era: 2 flutes (+ piccolo), oboe, 2 clarinets, bassoon, 2 horns, 2 cornets, 2 trombones, timpani, percussion and strings. According to Geoffrey Toye, the number of players in the Savoy orchestra was originally 31. Sullivan argued hard for an increase in the pit orchestra's size, and starting with The Yeomen of the Guard, the orchestra was augmented with a second bassoon and a bass trombone. Sullivan generally orchestrated each score at almost the last moment, noting that the accompaniment for an opera had to wait until he saw the staging, so that he could judge how heavily or lightly to orchestrate each part of the music. For his large-scale orchestral pieces, Sullivan added a second oboe part, sometimes double bassoon and bass clarinet, more horns, trumpets, tuba, and sometimes an organ and/or a harp. Many of these pieces used very large orchestras.

Sullivan's critical reputation has undergone extreme changes since he first came to prominence in the 1860s. At first, critics were struck by his potential, and he was hailed as the long-awaited great English composer. His incidental music to The Tempest received an acclaimed premiere at the Crystal Palace just before Sullivan's 20th birthday in April 1862. The Athenaeum wrote:

When Sullivan turned to comic opera with Gilbert, the serious critics began to express disapproval. Peter Gammond writes of "misapprehensions and prejudices, delivered to our door by the Victorian firm Musical Snobs Ltd. ... frivolity and high spirits were sincerely seen as elements that could not be exhibited by anyone who was to be admitted to the sanctified society of Art." As early as 1877 The Figaro wrote that Sullivan "has all the ability to make him a great composer, but he wilfully throws his opportunity away. ... He possesses all the natural ability to have given us an English opera, and, instead, he affords us a little more-or-less excellent fooling." Few critics denied the excellence of Sullivan's theatre scores. The Theatre wrote that "Iolanthe sustains Dr Sullivan's reputation as the most spontaneous, fertile, and scholarly composer of comic opera this country has ever produced." However, comic opera, no matter how skilfully crafted, was viewed as an intrinsically lower form of art than oratorio. The Athenaeum's review of The Martyr of Antioch declared: "It is an advantage to have the composer of H.M.S. Pinafore occupying himself with a worthier form of art."

Although the more solemn members of the musical establishment could not forgive Sullivan for writing music that was both comic and accessible, he was, nevertheless, "the nation's de facto composer laureate".

The Collaborative Pieces

All of these operas are full-length two-act works, except for Trial by Jury, which is in one act, and Princess Ida, which is three acts.

Thespis (1871)
Trial by Jury (1875)
The Sorcerer (1877)
H.M.S. Pinafore (1878)
The Pirates of Penzance (1879)
Patience (1881)
Iolanthe (1882)
Princess Ida (1884)
The Mikado (1885)
Ruddigore (1887)
The Yeomen of the Guard (1888)
The Gondoliers (1889)
Utopia, Limited (1893)
The Grand Duke (1896)

W.S. Gilbert – his Other Works

Poetry
The Bab Ballads, a collection of comic verse published roughly between 1865 and 1871
Songs of a Savoyard, London, 1890, a collection of Gilbert's song lyrics.

Short Stories
Foggerty's Fairy & Other Tales, a collection of short stories and essays, mainly from before 1874.

Some other short stories but not in the above appear here:-

Belgravia, Vol. 2 (1867). "From St. Paul's to Piccadilly," pp. 67–74
Fun, Vol. 1 new series (1865-1866) (several contributions by Gilbert; near end of volume)
Fun Christmas Number 1865, ("The Astounding Adventure of Wheeler J. Calamity,")
London Society, Vol. 13 (1868) (three "Thumbnail Sketches" by Gilbert)
On the Cards: Routledge's Christmas Annual (1867) ("Diamonds," and "The Converted Clown,")

Other Books
The Pinafore Picture Book, 1908, retelling the story of H.M.S. Pinafore for children, in prose narrative
The Story of The Mikado, 1921, a similar retelling of The Mikado for children

Plays and Musical Stage Works
Selected stage works that were important to Gilbert's career or were otherwise notable, in chronological order, excluding those listed under other headings below:

Dulcamara, or the Little Duck and the Great Quack (1866)
La Vivandière (1867)
Harlequin Cock Robin and Jenny Wren (1867), a Christmas pantomime.
The Merry Zingara (1868)
Robert the Devil (1868), it opened the Gaiety Theatre, London and ran in the provinces for 3 years.
The Pretty Druidess (1869), a parody of Norma – the last of Gilbert's five "operatic burlesques"
An Old Score (1869) (rewritten as "Quits!" in 1872) Gilbert's first full-length comedy.
The Princess (1870). Musical farce; the precursor to Princess Ida.
The Palace of Truth (1870).
Creatures of Impulse (1871), music by Alberto Randegger. From Gilberts story "A Strange Old Lady".
Pygmalion and Galatea (1871).
Randall's Thumb (1871). A comedy that opened the Royal Court Theatre.
The Wicked World (1873).
The Happy Land (1873). This work was briefly banned for its sharp satire of government ministers.
The Realm of Joy (1873).
The Wedding March (1873) a farce adapted from Un Chapeau de Paille d'Italie.
Rosencrantz & Guildenstern (published 1874, performed 1891). Gilbert's burlesque of Hamlet.
Charity (1874). Concerns Victorian attitudes towards sex outside of marriage.
Sweethearts (1874).
Tom Cobb (1875).
Broken Hearts (1875). The last of Gilbert's "fairy comedies", this was one of Gilbert's favourite plays.
Dan'l Druce, Blacksmith (1876).
Engaged (1877).
The Ne'er-do-Weel (1878); rewritten as "The Vagabond" after a few weeks.
The Forty Thieves (1878). Co-written with three other writers, WSG played Harlequin.
Gretchen (1879)
Foggerty's Fairy (1881)
Brantinghame Hall (1888) Gilbert's biggest flop, it sent producer Rutland Barrington into bankruptcy.
The Fortune Hunter (1897). Its reception provoked WSG to announce retiring from writing for the stage.
The Fairy's Dilemma (1904).
The Hooligan (1911).

German Reed Entertainments
Gilbert wrote six one-act musical entertainments for the German Reeds between 1869 and 1875. They were successful in their own right and also helped form Gilbert's mature style as a dramatist.

No Cards (1869)
Ages Ago (1869). Gilbert's first collaboration with Frederic Clay, ran for 350 performances.
Our Island Home (1870)
A Sensation Novel (1871)
Happy Arcadia (1872)
Eyes and No Eyes (1875)

Early Comic Operas
The Gentleman in Black (1870; music by Frederic Clay). The score is lost.
Les Brigands (1871), an English adaptation of Jacques Offenbach's operetta.

Topsyturveydom (1874; music by Alfred Cellier). The score is lost.
Princess Toto (1876; music by Frederic Clay). A three-act opera.

Later Operas (Without Sullivan)
Though not as popular as the works with Arthur Sullivan, a few of Gilbert's later works arguably have stronger plots than the last two Gilbert and Sullivan operas.

The Mountebanks (1892; music; Alfred Cellier). This is the "lozenge plot" that Sullivan declined to set on several occasions.
Haste to the Wedding (1892; music; George Grossmith). An unsuccessful adaptation of The Wedding March.
His Excellency (1894; music; Osmond Carr). Gilbert felt that if Sullivan had set it, the piece would have been "another Mikado".
Fallen Fairies (1909; music by Edward German). Gilbert's last opera, which was a failure.

Parlour Ballads
The Yarn of the Nancy Bell, with music by Alfred Plumpton. One of the Bab Ballads. 1869.
Thady O'Flynn, with music by James L. Molloy. 1868. From No Cards.
Would You Know that Maiden Fair, with music by Frederic Clay. From Ages Ago. c. 1869.
Corisande, with music by James L. Molloy. 1870.
Eily's Reason, with music by James L. Molloy. 1871.
Three songs from A Sensation Novel: "The Detective's Song", "The Tyrannical Bridegroom", and "The Jewel". 1871
The Distant Shore, with music by Arthur Sullivan. 1874.
The Love that Loves me Not, with music by Arthur Sullivan. 1875.
Sweethearts, with music by Arthur Sullivan. 1875.
Let Me Stay, with music by Walter Maynard. 1875.

Arthur Sullivan – His Other Works

Operas
The Sapphire Necklace (ca. 1863; unperformed)
Cox and Box (1866)
The Contrabandista (1867)
The Zoo (1875)
Ivanhoe (1891)
Haddon Hall (1892)
The Chieftain (1894)
The Beauty Stone (1898)
The Rose of Persia (1899)
The Emerald Isle (1901; completed by Edward German)

Incidental Music to Plays

The Tempest (1861)
The Merchant of Venice (1871)
The Merry Wives of Windsor (1874)
Henry VIII (1877)
Macbeth (1888)
Tennyson's The Foresters (1892)
J. Comyns Carr's King Arthur for Henry Irving (1895)

L'Île Enchantée (1864 ballet)
Victoria and Merrie England (1897 ballet)
The Window; or, The Song of the Wrens (1871 song cycle)

The Masque at Kenilworth (1864)
The Prodigal Son (Sullivan) (1869)
On Shore and Sea (1871)
Festival Te Deum (1872)
The Light of the World (Sullivan) (1873)
The Martyr of Antioch (1880)
Ode for the Opening of the Colonial and Indian Exhibition (1886)
The Golden Legend (1886)
Ode for the Laying of the Foundation Stone of The Imperial Institute (1887)
Te Deum Laudamus (1902; performed posthumously)

Overture in D (1858; now lost)
Overture The Feast of Roses (1860; now lost)
Procession March (1863)
Princess of Wales's March (1863)
Symphony in E, "Irish" (1866)
Overture in C, "In Memoriam" (1866)
Concerto for Cello and Orchestra (1866)
Overture Marmion (1867)
Overture di Ballo (1870)
Imperial March (1893)
The Absent-Minded Beggar March (1899)

Absent-minded Beggar (Rudyard Kipling) 1899

Arabian Love Song (Percy Bysshe Shelley) 1866
Ay de mi, My Bird (George Eliot)1874
Bid me at least Goodbye (Sydney Grundy) 1894
Birds in the Night (Lionel H. Lewin) 1869
Bride from the North (Henry F. Chorley) 1863
Care is all Fiddle-dee-dee (F. C. Burnand) 1874
Chorister, The (Fred. E. Weatherly) 1876
Christmas Bells at Sea (C. L. Kenney) 1875
County Guy (Walter Scott) 1867
Distant Shore, The (W. S. Gilbert) 1874
Dove Song (William Brough) 1869
E tu nol sai - see You Sleep (G. Mazzucato) 1889
Edward Gray (Alfred Tennyson)(1880
Ever (Mrs Bloomfield Moore) 1887
First Departure - see The Chorister (Rev. E. Munroe) 1874
Give (Adelaide Anne Procter) 1867
Golden Days (Lionel H. Lewin)1872
Guinevere! (Lionel H. Lewin) 1872
I Heard the Nightingale (Rev. C. H. Townsend) 1863
I Wish to Tune my Quiv'ring Lyre (Anacreon; trans. Lord Byron) 1868
I Would I were a King (Victor Hugo; trans. A. Cockburn) 1878
Ich möchte hinaus es jauchzen (A. Corrodi) 1859
If Doughty Deeds (Robert Graham of Gartmore) 1866
In the Summers Long Ago (J. P. Douglas) 1867
Let Me Dream Again (B. C. Stephenson) 1875
Lied, mit Thränen halbgeschrieben (Eichendorff)1861
Life that Lives for You (Lionel H. Lewin) 1870
Little Darling Sleep Again (Cradle Song) (anon) 1874
Living Poems (H. W. Longfellow)1874
Longing for Home (Jean Ingelow) 1904
Looking Back (Louisa Gray)1870
Looking Forward (Louisa Gray) 1873
Lost Chord, The (Adelaide Anne Procter) 1877
Love that Loves Me Not, The (W. S. Gilbert) 1875
Maiden's Story, The (Emma Embury) 1867
Marquis de Mincepie, The (F. C. Burnand) 1874
Mary Morison (Robert Burns) 1874
Moon in Silent Brightness, The (Bishop Reginald Heber) 1868
Mother's Dream, The (Rev. W. Barnes) 1868
My Dear and Only Love (Marquis of Montrose) 1874
My Dearest Heart (anon) 1874
My Heart is like a Silent Lute (Benjamin Disraeli) 1904
My Love - see "There Sits a Bird in Yonder Tree
My Love Beyond the Sea - see "In the Summers Long Ago"
None but I Can Say (Lionel H. Lewin)1872
O Fair Dove, O Fond Dove (Jean Ingelow) 1868
O Israel (Hosea) 1855
O Mistress Mine (William Shakespeare) 1866

O Swallow, Swallow (Alfred Tennyson) 1900
Oh Sweet and Fair (A. F. C. K.) 1868
Oh! bella mia - see "Oh! Ma Charmante"
Oh! Ma Charmante (Victor Hugo) 1872
Old Love Letters (S. K. Cowen) 1879
Once Again (Lionel H. Lewin) 1872
Orpheus with his Lute (William Shakespeare) 1866
River, The (anon) 1875
Roads Should Blossom, The (anon) 1864
Rosalind (William Shakespeare) 1866
Sad Memories (C. J. Rowe) 1869
Sailor's Grave, The (H. F. Lyte) 1872
St. Agnes' Eve (Alfred Tennyson) 1879
Shadow, A. (Adelaide Anne Procter)1886
She is not Fair to Outward View (Hartley Coleridge) 1866
Sigh no More, Ladies (William Shakespeare) 1866
Sleep My Love, Sleep (R. Whyte Melville) 1874
Snow Lies White, The (Jean Ingelow) 1868
Sometimes (Lady Lindsay of Balcarres) 1877
Sweet Day So Cool (George Herbert) 1864
Sweet Dreamer - see "Oh! Ma Charmante"
Sweethearts (W. S. Gilbert) 1875
Tears, Idle Tears (Alfred Tennyson) 1900
Tender and True (Dinah Maria Mulock) 1874
There Sits a Bird on Yonder TreeRev. (C. H. Barham) 1873
Thou art Lost to Me (anon) 1865
Thou art Weary (Adelaide Anne Procter) 1874
Thou'rt Passing Hence (Felicia Hemans) 1875
To One in Paradise (Edgar Allan Poe) 1904
Troubadour, The (Walter Scott) 1869
Village Chimes, The (C. J. Rowe) 1870
Weary Lot is Thine, Fair Maid, A (Walter Scott) 1866
We've Ploughed our Land (anon)1875
When Thou Art Near (W. J. Stewart) 1877
White Plume, The - see "The Bride from the North"
Will He Come? (Adelaide A. Procter) 1865
Willow Song, The (William Shakespeare)1866
You Sleep (B. C. Stephenson) 1889

Hymns (Title & First Line)
Adoro Te - Saviour, again to Thy dear name we raise (Arranger)
All This Night - All this night bright angels sing
Angel Voices - Angel voices, ever singing
Audite Audientes me - I heard the voice of Jesus say
Bethlehem - While shepherd's watched their flocks (Arranger)
Bishopgarth - O King of Kings, Whose reign of old
Bolwell - Thou to whom the sick and dying

Carrow - My God, I thank Thee Who has made
Chapel Royal - O love that wilt not let me go
Christus - Show me not only Jesus dying
Clarence - Winter reigneth o'er the land
Coena Domini - Draw nigh, and take the body of the Lord
Come Unto Me - Come unto Me, ye weary (Arranger)
Constance - I've found a Friend; oh, such a Friend
Coronae - Crown Him, with many crowns
Courage, Brother - Courage, brother, do not stumble
Dominion Hymn - God bless our wide dominion
Dulce Sonans - Angel voices, ever singing
Ecclesia - The church has waited long
Ellers - Saviour, again to Thy dear name we raise (Arranger)
Evelyn - In the hour of my distress
Ever Faithful - Let us with a gladsome mind
Fatherland (St. Edmund) - I'm but a stranger here
Formosa (Falfield) - Love Divine, all love excelling
Fortunatus - Welcome, happy morning!
Golden Sheaves - To Thee, O Lord, our hearts we raise
Hanford - Jesu, my Saviour, look on me
Heber (Gennesareth) - When through the torn sail
Holy City - Sing Alleluia forth in duteous praise
Hushed was the Evening Hymn - Hushed was the evening hymn
Hymn of the Homeland - The homeland, the homeland
Lacrymae - Lord, in this Thy mercy's day
Leominster - A few more years shall roll (Arranger)
Light - Holy Spirit! Come in might! (Arranger)
Litany (1) - Jesu, life of those who die
Litany (2) - Jesu, we are far away
Long Home, The - Tender Shepherd, Thou hast still'd
Lux eoi - All is bright and cheeful round us
Lux in Tenebris - Lead, kindly Light
Lux Mundi - O Jesu, Thou art standing
Marlborough - O Strength and Stay, upholding all creation (Arranger)
Mount Zion - Rock of Ages, cleft for me
Nearer Home - For ever with the Lord (Arranger)
Noel - It came upon the midnight clear (Arranger)
Old 137th - Great King of nations, hear our prayer (Arranger)
Paradise - O Paradise!
Parting - With the sweet word of peace (Arranger)
Pilgrimage - From Egypt's bondage come
Promissio Patris - Our blest Redeemer, ere He breathed
Propior Deo - Nearer, my God, to Thee
Rest - Art thou weary, art thou languid
Resurrexit - Christ is risen!
Roseate Hues, The - The roseate hues of early dawn
Safe Home - Safe home, safe home in port
St. Ann - The Son of God goes forth to war (Arranger)

St. Francis - O Father, who hast created all
St. Gertrude - Onward, Christian soldiers
St. Kevin - Come, ye faithful, raise the strain
St. Lucian - Of Thy love some gracious token
St. Luke (St. Nathaniel) - God moves in a mysterious way
St. Mary Magdalene - Saviour, when in dust to Thee
St. Millicent - Let no tears to-day be shed
St. Patrick - He is gone - a cloud of light
St. Theresa - Brightly gleams our banner
Saints of God - The Saints of God, their conflict past.
Springtime - For all Thy love and goodness (Arranger)
Strain Upraise, The - The Strain upraise in joy and praise
Thou God of Love - Thou God of Love, beneath Thy sheltering wing
Ultor Omnipotens - God the all terrible! King who ordainest
Valete - Sweet Saviour, bless us 'ere we go
Veni, Creator - Come Holy Ghost, our souls inspire
Victoria - To mourn our dead we gather here

Part Songs

The term "Part Song" is more usually applied to one where the highest part carries the melody with the other voices supplying the accompanying harmonies.

Also included here are the soprano duet, The Sisters, and the trio Sullivan composed for the play Olivia by W. G. Wills, Morn, Happy Morn.

O Lady Dear (Madrigal) - Composed 1857, unpublished.
It was a Lover and his Lass - Words by Shakespeare. Performed at the Royal Academy of Music, 1857, unpublished.
Seaside Thoughts - Words by Bernard Bartram. Composed 1857. Published 1904.
The Last Night of the Year - Words by H. F. Chorley. Published 1863.
O Hush Thee, My Babie - Words by Walter Scott. Published 1867.
The Rainy Day - Words by H. W. Longfellow. Published 1867.
Evening - Words by Lord Houghton, after Goethe. Published 1868.
Parting Gleams - Words by Aubrey de Vere. Published 1868.
Echoes - Words by Thomas Moore. Published 1868.
The Long Day Closes - Words by H. F. Chorley. Published 1868.
Joy to the Victors - Words by Walter Scott. Published 1868
The Beleaguered - Words by H. F. Chorley. Published 1868.
It Came Upon the Midnight Clear - Words by E. H. Sears. Published 1871.
Lead, Kindly Light - Words by J. H. Newman. Published 1871.
Through Sorrows Path - Words by H. Kirke White. Published 1871.
Say, Watchman, What of the Night? - Words from Isaiah. Published 1871.
The Way is Long and Dreary - Words by Adelaide Anne Procter. Published 1871.
Morn, Happy Morn - Composed for the play, Olivia by W. G. Wills. Published 1878.
The Sisters - Words by Alfred Tennyson. Published 1881.
Wreaths for our Graves - Words by L. F. Massey. Published 1898.

Fair Daffodils - Words by Robert Herrick. Published 1904.

Church Songs

By the Waters of Babylon - Composed c. 1850. Unpublished.
Sing unto the Lord - Composed 1855. Unpublished.
Psalm 103 - Composed 1856. Unpublished.
We have heard with our ears
(i) Dedicated to Sir George Smart and performed at the Chapel Royal, January 1860.
(ii) Dedicated to Rev. Thomas Helmore. 1865.
O Love the Lord - Dedicated to John Goss. 1864.
Te Deum, Jubilate, Kyrie (in D major) 1866.
O God, Thou art Worthy - Composed for the wedding of Adrian Hope, 3 June 1867. Published in 1871.
O Taste and See - Dedicated to Rev. C. H. Haweis. 1867.
Rejoice in the Lord - Composed for the wedding of Rev. R. Brown-Borthwick, 16 April 1868.
Sing, O Heavens - Dedicated to Rev. F. C. Byng. 1869.
I Will Worship - Dedicated to Rev. F. Gore Ouseley. 1871.
Two Choruses adapted from Russian Church Music, 1874.
(i) Turn Thee Again
(ii) Mercy and Truth
I Will Mention Thy Loving-kindness - Dedicated to John Stainer. 1875.
I Will Sing of Thy Power. 1877.
Hearken Unto Me, My People. 1877.
Turn Thy Face. 1878.
Who is Like unto Thee - Dedicated to Walter Parratt. 1883.
I Will Lay Me Down in Peace - Composed 1868. Published only in 1910.

Christmas Carols & Songs

Advent

Hearken unto me, my people - An Anthem for Advent or General Use. Words from Isaiah. (1877)

Christmas Carols

All this night bright angels sing - Words by W. Austin. (1870)
I Sing the Birth - Words by Ben Jonson. (1868)
It Came Upon the Midnight Clear - Words by E. H. Sears.
Part Song for Soprano Solo and Choir (1871)
Hymn Tune "Noel" (1874)
Upon the Snow-clad Earth (1876)
While Shepherds Watched - Words by Nahum Tate (1874)
Hark! What Mean those Holy Voices? - Words by John Cawood (1883)

Songs

Christmas Bells at Sea - Words by Charles Kenney (1875)

Two songs from The Miller and His Man - A Christmas Drawing Room Entertainment. Words by F. C. Burnand (1874)

The Marquis de Mincepie

Care is all Fiddle-dee-dee

The Last Night of the Year - Part Song - Words by H. F. Chorley (1863)

Chamber Music & Solo Piano

Scherzo - Piano Solo, 1857, unpublished.

Capriccio No. 2 - Piano Solo (unfinished), 1857, unpublished.

String Quartet - Performed at Leipzig, May 1859. Published 2000

Romance in G minor - For string quartet, 1859. Published 1964.

Thoughts - Two pieces for piano solo, Published by Cramer, 1862.

An Idyll - For Cello and Piano. Composed in 1865 and Published 1899.

Allegro Risoluto - Piano solo, 1866. Published only in 1974

Berceuse - Based on the theme of Hushed was the Bacon from Cox and Box but with additional material.

Day Dreams - Six pieces for piano solo. 1867

Duo Concertante - Cello and piano. 1868

Twilight - Piano solo. 1868

www.ingramcontent.com/pod-product-compliance
Lightning Source LLC
Chambersburg PA
CBHW060052050426
42448CB00011B/2420